THE
ULTIMATE
GUIDE TO
SUCCESS

T0117058

THE ULTIMATE GUIDE TO SUCCESS

Concentration

The Science of Success

Julia Seton, M.D.

MEDIA

MEDIA

Published 2020 by Gildan Media LLC
aka G&D Media
www.GandDmedia.com

THE ULTIMATE GUIDE TO SUCCESS. Copyright © JMW Group Inc. All rights exclusively licensed by JMW Group Inc., jmwgroup@jmwgroup.net.

No part of this book may be used, reproduced or transmitted in any manner whatsoever, by any means (electronic, photocopying, recording, or otherwise), without the prior written permission of the author, except in the case of brief quotations embodied in critical articles and reviews. No liability is assumed with respect to the use of the information contained within. Although every precaution has been taken, the author and publisher assume no liability for errors or omissions. Neither is any liability assumed for damages resulting from the use of the information contained herein.

Front cover design by David Rheinhardt of Pyrographx

Interior design by Meghan Day Healey of Story Horse, LLC

Library of Congress Cataloging-in-Publication Data is available upon request

ISBN: 978-1-7225-0334-5

10 9 8 7 6 5 4 3 2 1

CONTENTS

INTRODUCTION

The *Science of Success* was published in 1914. *Concentration*, the other book in this volume, was published first in 1909 and by demand reissued many times. These books were precursors of the self-help books such as those written by Dale Carnegie, Norman Vincent Peale and Napoleon Hill in the decades that followed. They have been selected for updating because their message is still meaningful to current day readers.

Dr. Julia Seton (1862–1950) was one of the most outstanding women of the late nineteenth and early twentieth century. She was one of the very few women physicians of her time, and one of the first women to be accepted into the American Medical Association. She devoted her life to helping people cope not only with their health problems, but also with the way they lived their lives.

Early in her career she recognized the close relationship between one's physical well-being and one's attitude toward life.

She was a pioneer in what today is called the holistic approach to healthy living. She was a leader in what was then known as the "New Thought" movement and gave lectures, wrote articles and books and formed a foundation to promulgate this concept.

The goal of the New Thought movement was to make people better and more efficient in whatever relation of life they may find themselves whether it be in their careers or their personal lives. The New Thought movement taught its followers to depend upon their own inner powers. It taught them to fulfill the place they were given (whatever that place may be) to the utmost of their powers and without fear, knowing that they have nothing to be afraid of and that within them are untapped levels of energy upon which they may call. In other words: New Thought reinforces the old common-sense doctrine of self-reliance, and belief in the integrity of the universe and of one's own soul.

Dr. Seton was a prolific writer. Her essays, articles and poems were widely published. In addition to the two books published in this volume, she wrote *Destiny, A New Thought Novel, Fundamental Principles of the New Civilization, The Key to Health, Wealth and Love.*

CONCENTRATION: THE SECRET OF SUCCESS

CONTENTS

Chapter 1
THE DESIRE FOR SUCCESS

Whenever the question is asked: "What is the world seeking? What the world wants most to secure?" the answer will most likely be that the whole world is seeking happiness. No matter how diverse or obscure the backgrounds of the respondents may seem, they all lead toward this one point, and everything in life combines to make for this one emotion.

In order to be happy, people must determine on what terms success is defined. When we find out from an individual what that person calls success, we have mastered the secret of the thing which will make that person happy.

We may ask a hundred different people what they mean by success, and we will get a hundred different answers. Webster defines success as, "favorable results; prosperity," and this is the definition which is generally accepted. Success, when rightly interpreted, means simply the power to do what we want to do. No matter what anyone else wants to do, or what that person might accomplish, that would not be our success. No one can really secure success except from one's own plane of comprehension. There are those who look upon money and the power to amass it, as the only true success; they might have anything else the world can give, and yet they would feel unsuccessful and cast down. Another may want love, and he or she might win honor, fame, money, yet missing love, the one thing truly wanted that person would be poor, unhappy, and unsuccessful. Success is a purely personal possession, and does not admit of a universal interpretation.

Granted that success really means getting what we want, and failure is the lack of power to do this, the next question which presents itself is, Why does not all of us, in every walk of life, get just what we want, when we want it and for as long as we want it? Why are we not all successful according to our plane of desire? This is the vital point, and the vital answer to it is, we are successful or unsuccessful through our own unaided law.

Success can be arranged for in every life, just as simply as can any other attribute of human existence.

It is an acknowledged fact that we have and express in ourselves just as much or as little as we have power to recognize and think possible of attainment. Success comes to us because we compel it. It does not wait around and then rush in without an accompanying effort on our own part. We achieve because we believe we can achieve, and we plan toward that end.

The physical world of competition is where some people look for what they call success and happiness, and on this plane many seem to be peculiarly subject to bad "luck." They are always working, striving, and never attaining. They are always "out of a job." If they go into business, they make a failure of it. If they take up any kind of occupation, they get sick and lose it. They are always poor. They live in lack, and every cell of their bodies evidences lack. The whole world is full of individuals who are always complaining of their "bad luck." They are never successful. This is the worldwide expression of unfortunate people. They never get anything they want, and they have always lived as strangers to happiness. It has never occurred to them that the whole thing is due to their own errors of position. They do not know that if they would look the whole world fearlessly in the face and ask for what they want and make no compromise, they would get it.

People who go at anything in a half-heated way, with the appearance and thought that luck is against them will always find that "luck" is against them; they make it so by their position toward it. No one will knowingly employ anyone who is a "has been," a "dead beat," or a "no good." The successful business executive wants employees who are "lucky," and whose zeal, courage, ambition, and belief in their own accomplishments make them a "mascot" for those who employ them. Every kind of work in the world is clamoring for "live ones," but there is positively no commercial value for the "dead ones" who glut the market.

There is a lot of difference between people who are "hunting a job" and those who are looking for work. Lots of people would "like a job" if they thought it did not mean work for them. They are looking for a nice, soft, easy place, where they can draw their salary without much exertion on their part. Those who want work are not long without it. If they know how to ask for it, they can secure anything that they want and keep it until they get tired of it or outgrow it, and then they can find another position just as easily. They are always happy, for they know how to get and keep what they go after, and they know that no one can take it from them but themselves. But people who are only hunting for a job are frequently out of work after they get a job, unless someone is constantly helping them.

The thing that makes the difference between successful and unsuccessful people is simply a difference of recognition of existing conditions, seen and unseen, and their own relation to these conditions. We have within us a vital power against which everything else is powerless, if we know it and know how to use it. This center is the powerhouse of our being, and here we attract and accumulate force; it is ruled over by our thoughts and our will.

We can attract anything in the universe to us on which we set our thoughts; we can then will it into position for transference to us. Thoughts are things, and whatever we "can think" we can become. We can fashion our own material universe by the simple correct control of our own thinking.

We cannot hope to vitalize anything into a successful termination or continuation for ourselves or for others, unless the torch of intense throbbing life burning within us. The consciousness of our own power lights the candle of the latent soul energy, and develops us along positive creative lines of application.

When we have thoroughly learned this lesson of our own power and control of the energy within, we become master over all external things. We have power then over all the negative forces in the universe. We are the highest expression of conscious power, and it is for us to command, they must obey.

People on the lowest round have within themselves the leaven of thought force that allows them to rise through their own increasing understanding. In concentration they have an open door nobody can shut. Concentration is not alone for those who are in specialized states of consciousness; it is the natural birthright of the laborer as well as the mystic. It is thought force centralized that produces form. Concentration creates not only the thing itself but the way by which that thing may be accomplished. There is nothing in heaven or earth, God or human, but spirit mind and spirit form. Through concentration we link ourselves with the true life, and from seemingly impossible conditions we can bring about the fruits of our powerful thinking and become lord ruler of our earthly domain.

It is our own fault if our lives narrow down to limitations, and our hopes to petty confines. It is our own fault if our work degenerates into the deadly routine of drudgery, in which we do always what others want us to do in order to build up their success, in which we can have little part. It is our own fault if we do not recognize our immortal birthright of freedom, but go on in paths where we hear only the death-knell of success and personal attainment.

It is not given to all to be equally great, or there would be no longer an expression of growth on this plane; but it is given to all of us to know the truth of our own latent possibilities and to develop them to the uttermost; to have high ideals and ambitions, and to work them out into the highest form of energy.

Chapter 2
THE NEED FOR CONCENTRATION

The first step towards conscious *concentration* is the power. Without concentration a life cannot expect to pass along in paths of peace. When we wish to know the difference between the physical, mental or psychical development of nations, races, countries or individuals, we can easily determine it if we look at the difference in their power of concentration.

Greece concentrated on art and beauty until she became a world of artistic wonder. Part of a nation concentrated for liberty, and the feet of the Pilgrim Fathers trod New England shores. A people concentrated for freedom, and the shackles of millions of slaves fell before them.

Concentration is the vital essence of all life, and without it there is no real purpose, no real control. Upon the power of concentration, more than upon any other one thing, depends our law of attracting, controlling and mastering life's conditions.

Everyone is born into this world in some direct line of concentration. One is not born an American, an Englishman, an

Irishman, a Jew, or a Chinese, by chance; everything comes by the laws of natural relationship. Each of us is just whatever we have made ourselves, through concentration, during our cosmic journey. We have built ourselves by the power of our own thought, and this thought energy is expressed in the objective conditions, in which we find ourselves,

Whenever we see an individual anywhere in life, whether successful or unsuccessful, from the Goulds, Vanderbilts or Rockefellers of the millionaire world to the common street-sweeper and rag-picker, we may be sure that they are, one and all, the direct result of their own creative energy, both inherited and acquired. We have a long line of millionaires on the one hand, and a long line of paupers on the other; we also have many lives that stand for success, power, and liberty of personal action. Besides these, there is a world full of failures and unfortunate expressions of lack. What has brought about these different expressions, and where did the division begin?

Long ages ago, when the thought or mind of these individuals began operating, the Law was there, as certain and unchangeable as life itself. We are all just the thing which our own concentration has made us, and it depends alone upon our own self whether we will go on, year after year, in paths that lead only to deeper and deeper lack; or whether we will face around, start new lines of powerful thought concentration which will lead us out from bondage into limitless freedom.

One day, on a street in Boston, I saw an old woman selling papers. Her hair was gray; her skin brown and wrinkled; her clothing shabby, and only half sufficient for the chill of the hour. She was simply poverty stricken, and her thin, piping voice trembled as she called her papers in an effort to compete with the crowd of newsboys around her. Many bought her papers, being drawn to her through sympathy and her evident need. I felt sorry that, with her gray hair, so near the grave, life should have only this to offer her. I sought a reason for it, and asked her to tell me her history.

She was the daughter of a minister. Her mother had been the proverbial meek little woman of history, perfectly fitted to be her father's wife. Her grandfathers, on both sides of the parental tree, had been ministers. She gave me a graphic sketch of the long line of concentration into which she had been born and in which she had continued. There was a long line of concentration for lowliness of spirit; for grace; for the utter sinking of self; lack of demand for place or power; lack of self-righteousness; absolute submission; sown through generations, sown by her in her own life, and it had to bring forth its fruit. It did it in the form of that gray-haired, beautifully ragged old woman, who in the last days of her declining years, gathered her harvest on the cold streets of a rich city, under-fed, poor and alone.

She was still true to her inherited concentration, for, while I questioned her, she said: "Health, money, and happiness are not for me. My family have borne the cross of poverty and sickness all their lives, and borne it nobly; and some day the Father will give us our reward."

It is not hard to see where her mind was poised and where that of her family had been poised for generations; nor is it hard to see the inevitable result from such a cause as that long line of concentrated thought force. They could not escape the effect of the Law they had built for themselves, and they will go on kissing their cross for generations yet to come, for their every thought is delaying their own possessions. She said: "Some day the Father will give us our reward," never knowing that the "day" was, by just that simple Law, put eternally beyond her, and that finally charity will feed her, clothe her, and bury her. All these are but the natural expression of the Law she set in motion for herself.

Then there is the story of the great composer Franz Liszt. His brother wanted to be a great landowner and own farm after farm, and scorned the musical inclinations of Liszt. Liszt would not share his brother's ambitions and ran away time after time to follow his desire for music. In after years, when the brother had by constant attention become a large and wealthy farmer and Liszt was still a poor, struggling composer, the farmer called on Liszt and, finding him out, wrote upon a card, "Herr Liszt, Land Owner." When, in the course of time, the composer returned the call and found his brother absent, he left his card with the inscription, "Herr Liszt, Brain Owner." Here are two examples of acquired concentration. Each followed his own line, becoming what he desired, although born under the same inherited concentration. One wanted land, concentrated, worked for, and obtained it. One wanted music, and the world today pays tribute to his concentration.

On these stories hangs all the truth of the Law. Whatever we wish to become, we may become, because no one says no to us but ourselves. No one limits us but ourselves. No one makes us pass along in paths of lack but ourselves. Whatever we have or do not have is a world picture, which we hang on our own life, and it tells everyone who runs and can read, the whole story of just how skillful or unskillful we are with the tools that were given us in the very dawn of our existence.

We are living hourly in a world full of glorious opportunities, and full of a substance from which we can fashion our own environment. There is no limit set for us, save the one our own understanding places upon us. We may have and hold and use all that there is, in just the hour we awaken to our own natural power of creation.

Our conditions, both in environment and body, are simply the product of our own consciousness. The rag picker is only this and nothing more, because this is what he has fashioned for himself from the substance of his own thought world,

He will remain a rag picker as long as he has only a rag picker's vision. As soon as he recognizes something better for himself, and sets about fashioning it by the power of concentrated thought and action, he will receive it.

Our thoughts are our creators, and they must create for us just what we direct them to create. It is no one's fault but our own if we set them to fashion a concentration of lack and limitation. The substance is always acted upon by thought force; and our homes, our friends, our bodies, our positions, everything, are only the outside picture of our inner self; and they are proof positive of the freedom or bondage of our own thought world.

We may be whatever we wholly desire to be, and our expression will follow us in form to the very limit of the power with which we plunge our consciousness.

The moment a life desires anything, it becomes related with that thing, and it has established the Law, which will bring it into union, if it knows how to fulfill the Law and then does it. Desire is the prophecy of its fulfillment, and when rightly directed, will bring to us even the things we have once called impossible, and then wisdom will make them our own.

Desire is the first out-reaching of the Law; it is the God-push within us trying to get us into relationship with the things, which the ALL LIFE has always had in store for us, waiting the hour of our unfoldment.

When we once learn the truth of the power of our own workmanship, the next step is to decide just what we wish to express and then set about fashioning it in consciousness. We are all discoverers, creators and unfolders. We must use all our tools to express ourselves. We first discover the plan of our life, and relate it with the Universal life. We must know what we want and know that it is ours, just as soon as we can manifest it. We always get our own on every level of consciousness. No Law can take our own away, because our own is whatever we have created for ourselves, and it belongs to us by the great cosmic law of having discovered the plan.

Once we have discovered the plan, we must then create it mentally. As conscious creators, we must always create the form in which we can express just what we want, and just how we want it, and then to create it in this form. The next step is to go on unfolding finer and finer expressions of the form; thus fulfilling the Law of constructive living.

Before we can discover, create, or unfold conditions to persist, we must first win control over our own minds, and consciously manipulate our own thought tools. We can never hope for an expression of power as long as we cannot control, direct and understand our own beings.

The unsuccessful lives are the non-concentrated lives. The sick minds are the abstract minds. The utterly helpless multitudes, that are always the object of charity, are those who have no concentration. They have fixed ideas of negativeness; and the puny plans they have discovered for themselves plunge them into constant relations with creations of lack, limitation and failure.

When thinking has not been passed into form, it is of little value in life; and when thinking does pass into form in our life, through unconscious, negative concentration, it can ruin us; but when thinking is consciously passed into a fixed power, and used for a powerful purpose, it can become the pathway to the very center of universal wisdom, and open the portals to divine discoveries and creations, which become the foundation for wonderful expressions in our life, and an aid to generations yet to come.

The first step on the path of Concentration is to own our own field of consciousness. Only about half the world does this. The entire sick world, the entire failure world, is owned by its own and other people's negative thoughts. It is interesting to notice how few there are who are really in control of their own minds. The field of consciousness is open to every kind of random, drifting thought forms; and many carry around minds that are ready to receive every negative thing that is projected into them either by individuals or conditions.

Often a thought will get possession of a mind and stay with it. Thoughts will pour in just as they please, bringing what they please, and the mind must accept them unless it is master of itself.

People will lie awake all night long, muse and brood all day over an unwelcome thought that possesses them, instead of owning their own field of consciousness and banishing the things which are only making them miserable.

The concentrated mind owns itself. It is the divine thinker of its own thoughts, and it declares just what kind of food the mind shall feed upon; it sets a guard upon its field of consciousness and will not allow a thought that is less than constructive to enter in. It picks up the thoughts which will reveal to it a perfect plan of life, then projects a perfect image of that plan and, standing firmly by its own creations, it fashions them again and again with increasing skill, until the whole structure of the self is brought into harmonious *at-one-ment.*

Our thoughts are tools, and the life substance is shaped with these tools. Every hour we can stand before our half-formed self and with tools a thousand times finer than those of the finest craftsman of the physical plane, we can cut, from our own thought atmosphere, forms of exquisite perfection, until body, environment, friends, even our whole life, is a world picture of peace, power, love, joy, health and wealth, limitless and free.

Thoughts must be taught to centralize in ideas; we must first pick out the thing we wish to fashion. If we want health, we must get the idea of health; we must think health thoughts and shut out the thoughts of disease by simply displacing them with the strong, positive idea of health. We must keep this thought of health before the mind until it becomes impossible to think disease. We fill our field of consciousness with the thought of the well, the strong, the powerful; the HEALTH of life. We force the pictures of hospitals, sanitariums, and sick people out of our minds. We create health in consciousness until the energy set in motion manifests in form. No matter how we appear, we look at ourselves, and we see only the perfect self; we hold this idea; we do not let a thought of anything else enter. At the start, other thoughts will attempt to enter, for we have not yet learned how to completely close the door in the face of unwelcome ideas; but as we go on centralizing in thought, we come to where we can hold the thought of whatever we wish as long as we wish; lay it down when we wish and take it up again when we are ready. Then we no longer fear the old thoughts when they do return, for under the power of concentration, no old thought can return more often than we can replace it with a new one of health and power. After a while the old negative ideas give way, having exhausted their own vitality, and are easily displaced forever by our new positive thought creations.

After we have learned to concentrate until we can hold one thought as long as we desire and have played with our own thought world and find that we are really the master of our own ideas, our next step is to begin to create the image and pass our idea into form. As long as we have only the idea, we have only realization; but when we can pass this idea into a perfect thought form, created from the indestructible thought substance of the universe, we are on the path towards actualization, and just a little more practice will make the things we have fashioned come from out the absolute and cluster around us in physical embodiment.

In order to create an image we must see the thought picture of the idea. If we have an idea of health, then we must lift ourselves aloft in a thought form of health. We must stand out in consciousness whole, vital, radiant; we must work on this thought picture until we walk right out into mental space, our whole being—body, flesh, tissue—glowing, gleaming and quivering with a health divine that will rise in our consciousness before it can ever be actualized in flesh and form. We must work on this creation until it is perfect.

No matter what our desire may be, we pursue the same plan. Whatever we expect to manifest in form we must first discover, create and unfold in consciousness. If we want wealth, we must always see the perfected plan of supply. The moment we can centralize and hold the desire, we are creating it, and if we know how to persist in this conscious imaging of our own creation, nothing in the whole world of Laws can keep it from fulfillment. This is the *one great law*, and it is too high for contradiction. As the bible so well states it: "As a man thinketh in his heart, so is he," and creation in consciousness is the reality of "thinking in our hearts."

After we have centralized in thought, then concentrated, then created, our next step is to "let go" and simply hold this conscious image, feeling and knowing that this great Creative Energy of the Universe is flowing through it, pushing it into form. There is nothing in this whole visible Universe that did not first stand complete in the thought world. The building lives in the mind of the architect; the song lingers in the heart of the composer; the acorn holds the energy that projects the oak; and humankind is no exception to the rule. But only as we know the power of the energy that creates can we become powerful in producing the things created.

When we have mastered the law of concentration we are lords of our own life. We then can be whatever we want to be. We are our own unaided law. We can soon learn to declare the Law under which our own life shall pass. Loss, failure, poverty, sickness and disease may indeed be real to the world around us, but they do not exist for us nor for those whom we can aid into the vision of the higher Law. We live to operate this Law for ourselves and for those who can comprehend it. Some lives turn away. They really do want health, wealth, love and peace, but the price of concentration and creation is too great; they want more to be undisturbed in their old thought habits.

Centralization in thought, concentration upon the thought, then creation in consciousness; this is the perfect Law of liberty. We can see ourselves and others in a new light. We begin then to pass the simple act of thinking into a fixed power, and we quit forever thought relationship with anything we do not want. We never spend one moment vitalizing into power anything that is not for our highest good. We pick out only the things which will make our life just what we desire, and we lift these things aloft in our thought world, projecting them consciously into form, and walk on serene and calm, undisturbed by any old thought force; knowing that our own must come to us, for we have created it for ourselves by our deeper wisdom. Negative things cannot exist for us in this new world of scientific spiritualized being.

This is not castle building; it is creation. In the old days, we built "air castles," knowing they must fall. We built them to fall; but in our new understanding we create a new condition. We build these conditions into the very heart of the Cosmic Law, and we build them to stand, for we know now the eternal truth that "With what measure ye mete it shall be meted unto you."

We have an immortal birthright to freedom and an abundant supply of everything. It is only the perverted thinking of the minds of men that has externalized lack in any form. Humanity must learn now the truth that no one limits us but ourselves, and that we get our supply simply by our own understanding.

Under the old Law we drifted along without concentration, mere puppets, acted upon by every random thought and condition, never knowing that we were free or bound, rich or poor, well or sick, happy or sad, successful or unsuccessful, not by our external but by our internal conditions. In the old thought, the things outside ourselves seemed real and beyond our control, and never likely to yield to our puny efforts. But now we know that humankind was never meant to be anything but master of all this lower kingdom; that we are the highest expression of all life here and now; that it is for us to command, and externals must obey. This is the Law, and there is no appeal from it.

We come into our kingdom in the hour we withdraw from the thought of the limitations of external things and manipulate them with the higher power of our own unfolded consciousness.

Union with the power of the Cosmic Life is a possible thing for every human life, and our personal expression is but the remote picture of our place in the Cosmos. Our concentration may become the very tree of life, and our conscious creations the fruit of our growing. We can choose this day what we will serve; the world is full of health and wealth and love.

Chapter 3
BREATHING AND CONCENTRATION

There are many textbooks on breathing; so many, in fact, that the student halts in a maze of wonder as to which to follow. They are all good, and each teaches some part of truth. There is nothing the developing world does half so imperfectly as breathing. Air is life; to breathe it is to keep ourselves alive, young, strong and vigorous on the physical plane; and on the subjective plane we can use our breath as a vehicle by which we reach the Divine life.

In many ancient cultures the breath is referred to reverently and with great appreciation. Words from various cultures indicate this truth. In Greek *pneuma,* breath moving in the body, gives us the word pneumonia, the Latin *spiritus* gives us inspiration and spirit (the non physical part of ourselves) In Hindu *atman*, the very feeling of God in the body. *Prana,* an Indian expression, means not only breath but also life force. In the Bible, God Himself *breathed* life into Adam. According to classical Chinese authors, the energies derived from Breathing represent the energies of Heaven; while the energies derived from food and water represent the energies of Earth. The breath is indeed a miracle.

Most people think breathing is a hard and strenuous task, and only to be accomplished after long and persistent application. It is hard to tell where this opinion had its origin; it is not true; never was and never will be. It is the most natural and simple thing in the world to breathe.

Because we breathe so many times during the day (about 20,000), it is easy to take breathing for granted. At night when we sleep we breathe automatically. We don't think about it, we just do it. Babies and small children breathe properly naturally but most adults breathe ineffectively. But making small adjustments in the way you breathe you can change your health and disposition dramatically.

It does not mean a violent gymnastic respiratory effort, persisted in indefinitely; nor an hour of shutting ourselves away from interruption; nor a going to the "mountain top"; nothing of the kind. It means just a simple in and out passage of the physical breath, done consciously and for a definite purpose. Just a breathing out of all the dead, worn-out things within us, and an inbreathing of all the vital, pulsing things which we desire, floated into our being through the connection of our breath life with the *all life* ether which encircles us.

We can make contact with the Universal supply of health, wealth, happiness, in fact, with everything we want, at any time in our everyday life, anywhere we may be at the time of our need. We can vitalize ourselves—inwardly and outwardly with this great creative energy just as easily when in a crowd of people, or hanging on to a strap in a crowded car, as we can if we were alone on a mountain top or locked in the seclusion of our own room.

There is one sure and certain way to make this connection with Divine supply, and one that every one may use and demonstrate as a good way. That is through *concentration*; thinking creatively of the thing we need, and then breathing ourselves into connection with it. We may concentrate forever, and if we do not place ourselves as a scientific link between our need and the supply, we will never make it ours. We hear people say, "I have concentrated for years; have never faltered in my thinking; have believed and worked and never laid down my hope, and yet today I do not make good my concentration, and I must believe that there is something wrong with this philosophy."

Where do these students fall down in their results? It is simply because they have worked entirely on the receptive side and have not created. The one, who desires and does not breathe to create his desires, is not really in *at-one-ment*. There is no other way of demonstrating our control and power except through the power of our breath. When we have learned the true science of the breath, we will never want for anything; but we will keep our concentration until, through this increasing development, we pass into that Divine knowledge of the spirit where we understand that we breathe the breath of life into our own nostrils. It is given us before we ask, but we must take it.

In our everyday physical world, our point of contact with physical things is our hands. If we want anything that is anywhere within our reach, what do we do? We don't sit down in hopeless despair and mourn, concentrate, hope and pray for it, and almost cry because it does not leave its present position and come to where we are. No, indeed; we just square ourselves for a big reach and, taking our position firmly, we reach out, clasp it with our hands, haul it bodily into place and put it just where we want it.

What our hands are on the physical plane, our breath may become for us on the subjective plane, if we learn how to use it consciously. The Laws of the subjective world are no more complex than are those of the objective, only the student does not understand the instruments of the subjective plane so well as be does those of his physical surroundings.

Concentration is the first step toward attraction and attainment. It places us in the correct position with the Universal forces, and makes it possible for us to get ready for a strong pull in the right direction. Have you ever seen a crowd of workers getting ready to hoist a heavy beam?

The leader gives the word to get ready. The workers all take their own point of vantage for a lift, and then with one strong, tremendous pull, the beam slowly swings into place. This is physical concentration; physical actualization. The concentration of the mind is the same; the reaching out of the breath is the same, only working with the invisible law of God, which is just as tangible on its own plane.

When we have placed ourselves, and concentrated upon the thing we want in the Universal supply, and breathed for it consciously and persistently, there is no more chance for it to escape us than there is for the beam to refuse to obey the strong physical strength of those who will it into place.

Long, deep physical breaths raise our bodily vibrations until we are enabled to unite subjectively with everything in the cosmic ether around us. When this union is perfect on both planes, we can draw into our environment everything we want.

It is better to concentrate on and breathe for one thing at a time, for not many of us are equal to the task of doing more than one thing at a time and doing it well. We can afford to let everything take its turn in our life; we do not have to hurry. Let us be sure we know what we want. We cannot make contact for actualization if we are halting and unformed in our desires. The Law exists to be fulfilled only for those who have power to command their own creations.

When we begin these creations, there will be times when we will feel that, in spite of our concentration, we have not connected. Our thoughts will not rise higher than our head, never mind; it is only because we have not yet succeeded in raising our physical vibrations. We can breathe ourselves on to the mountaintops of feeling, and after a while we will seem to pass on to any plane we wish. When our vibrations are equal on all planes, we become filled with a sense of eternal possession, and no longer recognize a condition as possible that can separate us from our desires.

A conscious rhythmical breathing, persisted in from day to day, will, and does, polarize us with the Universal supply and lift us in rapport with the great ocean of actualization. This is the Law; there is no appeal from it. The one who operates it consciously and powerfully, receives according to the degree he vitalizes it. The key to life is the Law. *Know The Law.* Get operation of the Law, and the rest follows just as naturally as the current runs along the wire.

Chapter 4

DIRECTIONS FOR BREATHING DURING CONCENTRATION

Wonderful power will manifest as a natural sequence to correct breathing. You should take from ten minutes to half an hour to concentrate, according to the rapidity with which your mind is capable of seizing and formulating ideas. During such concentration, decide which of the attributes necessary for development you most require, as each is a distinct force. Concentrate upon it in all its bearings; upon that to which you will devote its power when achieved. Make the desire impersonal as well as personal. Condense the subject of concentration into one word, if possible, or a very few words.

Many people over the centuries have practiced concentration by means of meditation. Some meditation gurus recommend that to concentrate, one should focus one's mind on a mantra, a sound that they will repeat over and over again during their period of meditation. Preferably it should be a sound that has no literal meaning, such as the humming sound "ommmmm."

By repeating this mantra over and over, the mind is released from all other thoughts and it can concentrate on becoming totally relaxed.

Meditation gurus like the Maharishi Mahesh Yogi, who advocated the practice of transcendental meditation, a movement that became very popular in the mid-twentieth century, would personally give each of his followers his or her own mantra, a Sanskrit word that he felt fit that disciple's personality.

Some people prefer using a word or phrase that has special meaning for them. It may be a biblical text such as a brief proverb or part of a prayer. Some Catholics recite *Ave Maria*—some the entire prayer, some just the two-word title. Some select a specific thought that sets the stage for them. One woman reported that by just saying over and over *Today is the day*, she reinforced the principle that "yesterday is past and gone, tomorrow has not come, it is today that I must live now."

Select a mantra that best suits you. Make it part of your breathing exercise. Breathe in, repeat the mantra, as you breathe out—over and over again.

When concentration is ended, commence movements by placing yourself in as tranquil a mood as possible. With every inhalation, think the word or words, which are the subject for concentration. When inhaling, hold yourself positive, except in such cases as will be mentioned later; that is, hold the purpose of retaining and assimilating the force desired. Try to realize that with every inhalation you are in reality drawing, from an unlimited supply, the needed force. This can only be accomplished by faith, in the beginning; but gradually you will realize that you are becoming stronger, and faith will give way to knowledge, and you will see that you are literally drawing into yourself the energy that creates and which must ultimately give the desired power. Every spiritual, as well as material idea, object or attribute, exists primarily as energy in the Universal Mind and is capable of being attracted by individually developed minds into their aura to augment its kind, and there remains to be dissipated in form, according to the power and development of the individual.

If the idea of health should be chosen, consider yourself as perfectly healthy, harmonious, symmetrical; in fact, just as you would desire yourself to be as regards health. If some particular organ is affected, hold the image of a perfectly healthy organ in your mind while thinking the word and breathing.

When you desire to send some requisite force to another person, hold yourself as an instrument through which that force may be disseminated; drawing it to yourself, by inhalation, releasing and directing it by exhalation; holding yourself positive in exhalation. Never send anything but an impersonal force. Remember that nothing comes back to you but the things you send out, so be very careful of your creations. Make every conscious creation one of health, wealth and love, both for yourself and all others.

Some students require considerable practice to enable them to concentrate upon one word or sentence throughout the series of movements, but gradually the power will be attained. Remember that not only this life, but many others have been given to the negative creations, and you cannot expect to undo in a day that which has taken centuries to accomplish; so be patient with yourself. Remember that "we build the ladder by which we rise from the lowly earth to the vaulted skies, and we mount to its summit round by round."

Chapter 5
BREATHING EXERCISES

1. All inhalations should be made through the nostrils; all exhalations through the mouth. Stand evenly on the bottom of both feet, with hands hanging at sides. Draw in the breath slowly, while raising hands outward and upward until backs of hands touch above the head. Then slowly exhale air, letting hands fall until first position is resumed.

2. Stand with hands raised above the head, palms out; exhale while lowering hands and describing half circle, touching toes as nearly as possible without bending knees. Inhale slowly, raising hands, resuming first position.

3. Hold arms at sides; while inhaling, slowly raise right arm until perpendicular. While exhaling, lower right arm and raise the left. Then inhale again, and while inhaling, lower left arm and raise the right as before, and so on.

4. Stand upright and bend from the waistline, first to the right, as far as possible, then to the left, in same manner. Inhale while bending to the right, exhale while bending to the left.

5. If you have any organic disease, do not take this exercise without consulting a physician. Inhale slowly, drawing in until the lungs are filled and the abdomen extended as far as possible. Retracting abdomen, exhale until the organs are in a normal position.

6. Fill the lungs slowly; when filled, exhale as quickly as possible in three spasmodic movements.

7. Inhale as quickly as possible, and exhale slowly in three spasmodic movements.

8. Stand upright with arms hanging; while inhaling, bend the body from hips slowly forward as far as possible. Exhale as you straighten up and bend back. A weight or dumbbell, weighing from two to five pounds, may be held in each hand when it is desirable to increase muscular action.

9. Lie down on the floor, feet together, and arms at sides. Fill the lungs with air, and hold it until you have twice raised and lowered your arms above your head horizontally, touching the backs of the hands together. Exhale slowly as the arms lower the last time.

10. Take a full breath, while lying on the floor; extend the arms full length perpendicularly in front of the chest; touch hands; open arms until hands touch floor on either side of you, twice. Exhale while bringing arms up the last time.

11. Still lying on the floor, inhale while raising the right leg until it is as nearly as possible perpendicular with the body. Exhale while raising right and lowering left in the same manner; repeat.

12. Still lying on the floor, inhale slowly, drawing in until the lungs are filled and the abdomen extended as far as possible. Retracting abdomen, exhale until the organs are in a normal position. If you have any organic disease, this exercise should not be taken until you have consulted a physician.

The movements of each exercise should be made from five to twenty times.

After you have fully mastered the breath you can drop these physical exercises; taking simply the thought, projecting the image, and pass directly into the silence. *Breath, concentration, silence*; this is the trinity of creation. The Cosmos knows its own Laws; from it is our human life born.

Chapter 6
DIRECTIONS FOR CONCENTRATING

Your first step is physical silence. Sit or stand in a comfortable position and get perfect relationship with your body. One cannot go far in centralization or creation, when an uncomfortable foot, hand, or chair demands attention. Get right, on the physical plane first, before you start to find other levels of consciousness.

The next step is to centralize in consciousness. Stop diverse thinking. Pick up one thought, no matter what, and hold the mind to it as long as possible. Try this over and over until the mind will keep to the one thought from five to ten minutes. If the thought of health is chosen, think health; of all it would mean; what use it would be; what we mean by health. Think of it in all its details; work out a fine understanding of just what health is and what it means to possess it. *If the mind wanders, or other thoughts drift in, displace them again and again with the conscious thought of health, until only the health thought remains.* Whatever word is taken for centralization, practice with it until it can be held to the exclusion of any other thought, before passing on to the next step of conscious imaging.

After having centralized, the next step is to build these thoughts into form. If the thought has been health, we begin to see the self just as we want it to be. Every life knows just how it wants to be. Everyone has a divine image, which their higher consciousness holds before them, whispering just what they may become. Find this image, and live and luxuriate in the belief that it is manifesting now. We try to see ourselves perfect at once. This is imaging wholeness, but if we cannot see wholeness all at once, take up one thing at a time. First take that which we believe is the least perfect and see it whole. No matter what it is, see a perfect image, and be blind to anything less than this perfect image.

Creation in consciousness comes slowly to some students. The old distorted self will intrude negative ideas again and again into the thought world; but after repeating this creation powerfully for a while, the act of consciously imaging wholeness becomes easy, and no time is needed to project a perfected image. At each concentration the image can be worked upon, and each time it will become more perfect.

Conscious imaging is the greatest secret of the present age. It has always been used since mind began, but in the past it was used without a full understanding of its power. The Metaphysicians, Hypnotists, Suggestive Science teachers have always included it in their methods, but were unconscious of its real value and never instructed their patients in its deep spiritual meaning.

There is not an hour of our life that we are acting without an image. Every thought, every word, carries with it the form.

If some one speaks the word "rose," we at once see some kind of a rose. We do not see a tulip or any other kind of a flower, but something that we have called a "rose" immediately takes form in our mind. We cannot read a poem or a story, but our mind follows form in picture projection. "Some day I'll wander back again to where the old home stands; beneath the old tree, down the lane, afar in distant lands." What do we see? Read this quotation again and think about the picture our idea centers project. It is not hard to see it.

Just as the teacher of drawing reads a story to the class and then has each one draw just what his or her idea centers registered; just so is Life always telling us a story, and we are pushing out into consciousness the forms we have power to project.

There are some minds that are full of negative images. Their whole field of consciousness is lined with distorted thought forms of poverty, lack, disease, fear, shanties and hovels, built for themselves in consciousness and revitalized every day by their own energy; then they turn with puny questioning and wonder why their objective life is hourly taking on the same expression. We must learn this lesson, that just what we project into form in consciousness cannot refuse to manifest for us in our external world. We must know that we can never expect perfect manifestation from imperfectly formulated thought images.

Some of our first images must, through ignorance, be very crude. So are the artist's first pictures; or a poet's poems; or a composer's songs; or an architect's plans. But as we go on mastering the art of creating in consciousness, we grow more and more perfect, until we can really build a "temple not made with hands, and a house eternal in the Heavens."

After we have centralized and created, then the next step is the Silence. This is where we make our own life the link between the great creative spirit of the Universe and the thing we have created. "Through life comes life," and when we have finished our work and rested in this infinite energy, we make our own life the scientific link between the energy that creates and the thing we have created, and it flows through us, vitalizing our creations into form.

We remain in this silence, knowing "It is finished," until we feel the return of active thoughts; then we come again to our common human life, and walk on, expecting hourly to meet the things which we have projected.

First just an abiding knowledge of the thing we want. Just a conscious projection of a perfect image; beatific; glorified; just a consciousness of Infinite supply. Just a holding of our own thought world steadily as a flame glows; then walking on each day in calm security; turning again and again into peaceful at-one-ment with our source. This is the pathway of the strong; the whole, the useful. Their life is the light of the world.

Chapter 7
DIRECTIONS FOR GOING INTO THE SILENCE

In the beginning it is essential to be alone. You should have a time and place in which to begin the exercises. The first thing is to take a comfortable position, either standing, sitting or lying down, as may best suit you; then choose the attribute you wish to develop and take from ten to fifteen minutes to concentrate on it. Think of it in all its details; just what possession would mean to you; create it from the mental attitude of interior possession. If health is chosen, see yourself just as you would be. No matter what subject may be chosen, always see the perfect interior expression of it. Never build anything but a perfect image, and feel that it is capable of being materialized.

The next step is to begin the in breathing of long, deep breaths, and at every breath you should feel and know that you are really drawing to yourself from an inexhaustible supply, everything you desire; and you really are for every material as well as every spiritual thing exists as force in the universal energy and is capable of being attracted into especially developed auras and there lifted aloft in form.

After you have concentrated and established a rhythmical breathing, you should feel that it is finished, and then proceed to pass into the great creative silence, where the thing created becomes vitalized with an indestructible energy.

The last step is to withdraw the mind from the external world; to relax and live in the full consciousness of power, and this is accomplished by assuming a listening attitude. Get quiet-quiet—and still more quiet. Listen—listen; this is the way to the center of being; listen—listen—listen; so deep that you can hear your own heart beat. When you can hear the beating, or even feel fully the vibrations of your blood pulsing through your heart, you have come close into the universal rhythm and are awake in the supra-consciousness of your own mind, and you are ready to make the great creative cosmic union.

In this atmosphere we create by just the act of recognition; we *know* that we *are*. This is not thought force; it is revelation. We retain this consciousness of infinite union until every fiber of ourselves passes from the state of "becoming," into "being." Then we have finished our silence for that time, and can return to take up the common consciousness of our daily life. We now find ourselves strong, vital, and vibrant with a new power that was secured in this state of spiritual chemicalization.

Some lives seem to take a long time to develop to this point of understanding; but it is not really a hard nor wearisome task to find the center of being within us. The perfect rhythm of the breath should be established during concentration, so that when we go into the deeper consciousness the breath may take care of itself. It will be useless to attempt to awaken the supra-conscious mind if the breathing is tense, or demands conscious attention or control. The physical breath is only the expression of divine atmosphere, and once the physical rhythm is established, no more attention need be given to it; breath on the higher plane is simply life. It is only the soft, natural, deep passing in and out of the physical breath, done first consciously and for a definite purpose, then relinquished and carried on by natural relationship.

It is not a strange, mysterious, metaphysical thing, this going into the silence; but a sane, scientific, tangible truth, which anyone who cares to know may demonstrate for himself, and the inevitable outcome of it is perfect development; is *wholeness*.

Just a moment of powerful concentration; just a moment of stillness, deep as life itself; just a moment of conscious infinite union, and our human mind becomes the perfectly adjusted wireless instrument that registers the cosmic intelligence and secures its messages.

Remember, a concentration so full of force that it is alive; an inbreathing of cosmic energy; then stillness so intense that we touch the cosmic heart; then supra-conscious recognition of our *oneness*. Our being is then flooded with a divine power, and we become "as one who walks a pathway fashioned from the stars, and sheds his light about him as he goes."

Chapter 8
THE TRUE SILENCE

Where do we go when we go into the Silence? Not many students really know. They have a confused idea of stillness, but beyond the plane of physical silence, few there are who have any real conscious correspondence.

The silence is simply the functioning of the supra-conscious mind, and is a condition normal to everyone. It is capable of being brought into expression by those who know the true laws of their own minds.

There are three states of consciousness with which each individual may become familiar. The first is the common mind, or that part of the mind that is always busy with the external world and its laws. The second is the subconscious mind, or the mind of the psychic self. This is simply the film of the camera behind the lens of the objective or common consciousness or mind. The third is the supra-conscious mind, and is simply that part of the consciousness with which we contact the higher etheric vibrations and register them in the psychic mind, to be used as thought force in our common mind.

We can live at will in each one or all of these states of mind; and we are known by the amount of power we express in them all. We all know people who have no correspondence with any of them except the common consciousness. They give us a distinct picture of their personal selves; the exaltation of their personal egos is too plain to be mistaken. They are knowers of things; manipulators of the world of form. They live in a material world, in a material body with five material senses, and everything outside of their common mind and its functions they call a fad, a freak, or something visionary. They are normally related to the physical universe, and they stay normally related until, by the great cosmic law of evolution, something stirs within their beings that let them know there are still some things they do not know.

The psychic or sub-conscious mind is that state of consciousness formed by the union of the common and supra-consciousness. It does not exist in itself; it is the function of the psychic self; and it keeps intact all that is given it. It pours these records back into the common mind whenever anything stimulates it into action.

One who is living in the control of the psychic self and its mind, is introspective, abstract, incoherent, and often useless. This part of the mind should only be used as a storehouse in which the experiences of life are kept.

The supra-conscious mind is that state of consciousness which registers the higher cosmic vibrations. It is the wireless station that catches the universal messages. It is always receiving and sending out radiant energy; vitalizing both the common and sub-conscious mind with power. When we know the truth of the existence of this function of our own mind, we have indeed found the "well of water" within ourselves from which we can drink, and it becomes in us a "well of water springing up into everlasting life."

Most students, in their first attempts to get into the Silence, never get farther than the place where they go to sleep. This is a natural action of the common mind, for its function is to deal with thoughts, and when it is no longer needed to do this, its next function is to sleep. In order to go on, the student must first master the art of stilling the common mind and yet keep it awake. After this is accomplished he or she is ready to find the sub-conscious state.

When we reach the sub-conscious or psychic mind, we at once becomes auto-hypnotic, and feel an inclination to remain in a half sleeping and half waking state. We grow more and more introspective and subjective, until all subjective sense is lost. This is as far as some students ever get. They stay there luxuriating in subjective fancies and visions, returning to the common consciousness without ever having sensed the truth of the other state of power lying just a little further on.

Just as we must conquer the habit of sleep in the common mind before we can find the true subjective self, so must we conquer the habit of visions, vibrations and introspection of the sub-conscious mind before we can feel the real power of the supra-conscious mind. The one who stops on the psychic level of consciousness of the sub-conscious mind, will forever remain a babe in wisdom beside the one who, knowing the Law, sets out to find its full expression.

When we have awakened the psychic or sub-conscious mind, then we shall touch the supra part of our consciousness, and this is a place of absolute cessation of physical sensation.

It is action of mind so high that it appears to be motionless and thoughtless. It is higher than the human thought production, and it comes surging through the being simply as energy. It is only momentary, and it touches as a flash of lightning, so quick and so intense is its expression; but the mind that touches it never forgets; and once touched, it can be touched again, until after a while we can still our common mind, waken our psychic or sub-conscious mind energy, and contact with the supra mind at will, and then, turning to the world life around us, our daily lives will take on a power unknown by those who have only the contact of the common, or even the sub-conscious or psychic mind.

When we have made the common, the psychic and the supra mind *one*, and operate them all from the spiritual power of the supra mind, we have returned to our. Source and we can sink our string of thought into the fathomless, for we are really "grappled to the rock of ages."

THE SCIENCE
OF SUCCESS

CONTENTS

KNOW THYSELF

The building of a beautiful perfected selfhood is the work of every life; no matter what we do, whether we call it good, bad or indifferent, it is all directed towards this purpose.

Every inaction or action pushes us on into finer selection of material, which will serve to perfect ourselves.

Everything, which we contact, becomes legitimate material from which we can select or reject.

There is nothing, which can be eternally rejected; whatever is passed up at any place in our unfoldment becomes material to use at another place on the path. There is only one substance and we as master builders, can insert just what we see fit at any place in the construction of our plan.

In this building we must make selections so that the results of these selections will be continuous and whatever takes on permanency is called success, and whatever is called failure; is only one part of the great law of success and is success manifesting negatively.

You can ask a thousand people what they call success and they will give you a thousand different answers. Some call money success and the ways and methods which will unite them with money, the power to manipulate these laws and to select and retain all the material which produces a continued expression of opulence, they do not seek to select or unite with anything else in the self because this is the lesson their souls have come to include. There are others who count health and the power to manifest their consciousness through a perfect physical medium, success—they give their whole time to selecting the time, the place, the methods and materials which will build for them normal, physical and mental conditions allow them the unlimited action of a body that is free from pain. They select or reject one thing after another and call themselves successful in the degree that they secure this fulfillment and they weep and complain when they do not accomplish it, not knowing that disease is just as great a factor in the production of God-consciousness as health is.

There are many who call human love success, and they keep their human senses drugged with the narcotic of this race belief: they count themselves successful and go on each day rejoicing in their idol, and in just the degree that they demonstrate human love they feel they have made a success of their lives. When they fail in this and have to walk the pathway of life alone, uncompanioned, save by the crowd, they send forth a cry of sorrow and of failure, alone and not lonely is a part of the law of The One.

There are others who hold success to be such material and methods as will link them in a great law of service to the race, they count the opportunity to give of their time and supply to others as the greatest success possible for them, and in the degree that they can select place and opportunity to serve the world they feel they are successful, but if they have to stand idle while every pulse is throbbing to serve, they again, send out the cry of failure and feel like a cast off atom and they join the mighty army of complaint that they are wasting their time, they never realize that one of the highest laws of consciousness is that "they also serve who only stand and wait."

New Thought looks at all these evolving degrees of race consciousness and strikes for it a higher note of understanding, it in a way that it was never answered before, and then it follows this with scientific instructions of how to attain that thing which the mind designates as success.

We see clearly that all of us are doing just the thing we should do and that when we have gotten enough of the old thing and includes all its laws in our consciousness we will quit and naturally pass on into the inclusion of something else.

All of us are doing the very best we know how to do with our time, opportunity, and materials. If we knew better we would do better, and New Thought seeks only to increase our "know how." It does not condemn, it does not control, it does not punish, it only points the way to larger powers and privileges and better materials from which we may select or reject and through which we may express a higher self-hood. Success is the power in each of us to get the thing we want, when we want it, in the way we want it, to keep it as long as we want it and when we have included it, let go of it, and pass on to the fulfillment of a new desire.

There are those who have the power to get the thing they want and after they have quite outgrown the desire and included all that it can bring them, they are obliged to go on day after day, clinging to the dead body of their old desire. This is not success—this is failure; it takes its part indirectly in the fashioning of success, for on every step of their pathway they are learning in this way, the higher mastery and control that is necessary for them to know, and every ounce of power generated on this plane of failure, takes its place in the constructive work of the next step.

The power to get what we want when we want it and then pass it up constructively, and go on to another want, is not won by a moment's contact with people, conditions or things, but it comes as the result of slow self mastery and comradeship with all forms of human experience.

Success is not a mysterious, metaphysical thing that waits around and then rushes unannounced in to a life, but it is a sane, sensible entity, born from the consciousness of high power.

Success is the product of success methods and recognition of universal laws and it comes and abides with us in just that hour when we compel it.

There is no such thing as good or bad luck. We create these conditions within our own consciousness and develop them into form by our thoughts and actions.

There are thousands of well-defined success methods and the one who possesses the greatest number of these methods and uses them will be the greatest success.

The first success method includes all success but only a few people are clever enough to manifest this success method without further interpretation.

This first success method is: "Know Thyself." When we really know ourselves and all that the self means, we are straight in the middle of the divine channel of life, and can steer our boat from end to end of the channel without fear of shipwreck, but among the great failure multitude there is only one in a thousand who has any idea of this law.

You can ask the vast multitude of the unemployed or you can ask anyone who tells you a story of bad luck and who is weeping and moaning over their failures, and they have no idea of their place or use in the universal plan.

The old civilization lumped the whole race off in one confused bundle of states of mind and never gave it an idea of the legitimate plan of universal progress, or what part they must individually bear in the responsibility of this plan.

New Thought divides humanity into four planes of expression, namely, Body, Mind, Soul and Spirit. We function through the body in *instinct*, through the mind in *reason*, through the soul in *emotion*, and the Spirit in *intuition, revelation* and *prophecy*.

All of us have one or two and sometimes all of these planes in expression and we have success or failure in just the degree that we know ourselves and contact consciousness from our own plane of power.

A plane of consciousness is only a state of being in which we live, and through which we have our own individual law of transference; and a complete understanding of these planes of consciousness and their laws makes us masters of ourselves and of life in all its forms. It has taken generations of thinking to at last evolve this truth that every life is named, numbered, chorded and placed in its own natural law of attraction, and when it works in unison with this law it has success, when it works in opposition it has failure.

When we have found ourselves and our natural contact, we are straight in the middle of the Divine channel of success and rowing with the full force of the tide in our favor; but where we do not know ourselves, we are rowing against the tide or drifting idly and at every moment we are dashed against the rocks of error in the channel.

It has been written "God has provided some better things for us, that they without us cannot be made perfect." This is true. "Know thyself" is the first step toward becoming one with the things provided—then life will ask and answer its own questions.

PLANES OF EXPRESSION

We divide people into four planes of expression, namely: body, mind, soul and spirit, and they function through these in instinct, reason, inspiration and intuition.

Body Plane. Purely physical people are found among farmers, laborers, peddlers, miners, laundry workers, or any group of people that work under close supervision. Arrangement and order are not necessary. Also in this category are those who simply love the creature comforts, and who want all sense satisfaction, but do not want to go to any exertion to get it.

Mind Plane. Men and women in the lower mental plane are the straw bosses, the carpenters, contractors, train conductors, dressmakers, milliners, cooks, heads of departments in large stores, small store-keepers—and any type of person who works at physical labor that has some little show of order, adjustment and creative ability.

Higher Mental Plane. These men and women are the professors, school teachers, chemists, lawyers, engineers, secretaries, stock brokers, musicians singers who have cultivated voices but with no evidence of soul and others who have skill and management which make for success in material things.

Soul Plane. The soul plane is divided into two expressions, higher and lower. On the lower soul plane we have the professors, doctors, teachers, organizers, dentists, lawyers, nurses, managers of institutions, the heads of sanatoriums leaders of philanthropic movements, and others who work in many humanitarian expressions of life

The higher soul plane, in both men and women, is characterized by high ideality, vivid imagination and extraordinary inspiration. Here we find artists, writers, authors, composers, singers, elocutionists, and writers of drama.

Spirit Plane. Here we get into the world of religion. This includes preachers, evangelists great philanthropic leaders, religious organizers, higher educational workers, the inventor, the great composer, improvisers and the tragedians of the drama. People on this plane see everything by faith. Their intuition is their guide, and they find it hard to materialize all their ideas and visions into material expression.

Union of planes. This is the creative positive life. It expresses itself in instinct, reason, inspiration and intuition. It is usually found to have a fixed point of attachment on one plane, but it passes to the others at will. We have in this plane the statesman, the great leaders of social and religious science; also the masters of physical expression, such as contortionists, equilibrists, investigators, and organizers of great companies. Also landscape gardeners. This latter class know beauty, art, arrangement and physical laws of equalization, and through the perfect understanding of the laws of being, every life may control its development and make for unqualified success.

If we hope for success in all our undertakings, we must have our whole understanding founded upon the full power of our own genius in the line of least resistance. A business manager hoping for success could not afford to send an intuitional person to buy real estate, and take his or her opinion on trust as to the likely value; the judgment of such a person would not be reliable in material things. Any one in business who does these things courts failure and not success. Again, if some one contemplating a vacation tour desires to go to the most beautiful and wonderful scenery and to a place which would mean rest, inspiration and healing, it would not be wise to send as an advance agent one who was purely on the mental plane. Such a person would bring back time-tables, hotel facilities and locations, but nothing of the things which really should be known. Mental things demand mental recognition, and soul and spirit things demand their own cognizance. Flesh and blood only reveal physical and mental things; the great subjective things remain obscure until revealed by subjective consciousness.

The reason so many are seeking success, fame, money, love and recognition and not finding it, is because they have never learned the first necessary lesson of knowing themselves. First, they do not know what they want to do, and secondly, they do not know how to do what they want to do. They go on in aimless drifting and come at last to be some of the driftwood of life which is washed up onto the shore as the stream of success and failure flows on.

There is work and pay for all, success for all, in just the hour we know ourselves and connect with it. When one wants to be a farmer go among farmers; musician, among musicians; commercially oriented people, among the marts of trade, and so on. If we have within ourselves, a fully fledged consciousness of our own indwelling power, nothing can keep us from dragging out from the Universal Supply Company the things which belong to our own life.

The first true law for success is know to what part of the mighty system of the universe you belong, and then strike boldly out in that current of life. If you find that you respond to all that, physically, mentally, emotionally and intuitionally, you are vibrant with life, Then you can choose the things which you like best.

The creative life can do more than one thing at a time and do them all well. Just keep inside your own power of concentration; the creative life does not think in time, it thinks in eternities; it does not think in states, it thinks in continents; it does not think in dollars, it thinks in millions, and as long as it holds its mental mastery all things fall before its power.

If you are only developed in one direction and in one plane of consciousness, then plunge your desire in that direction; get the work that fills your whole heart and stick to it, and put into operation every day all the fundamentals of New Thought, and if you do this, you will not be a failure, for you can think yourself straight into the very center of supply, and whatever you command to become your own will come and manifest for you. With the knowledge of what you really can do, of just where you belong in the divine plan, and a consciousness of your latent energy and ability, you are straight in the middle of the road of success and it will never turn you one single step out of the way of peace, power and plenty.

HAVE A PLAN

After we have found ourselves and adjusted harmoniously in our own plane of expression we may find that we are still not manifesting sufficiently the degree of success desired, and strive as we may, we cannot discover where we are going off the center of the law.

Sometimes it takes a deep perception to find that we are breaking the next essential and usually breaking it because we do not know that it is the next important thing in the Science of Success.

This next all-important essential is Order. Order is God's first law and humankind's first law is obedience to this law; order is expressed in the form of a plan. "Have a plan," this is the second fundamental of success, for without a plan the human side of life must be always out of order and drift like a rudderless boat.

The whole failure world has this law of the lack of order somewhere in operation. There are thousands of planless, aimless, purposeless people everywhere. You can ask them "What do you want?" and they tell you that they have a profound idea of what they want to do and believe in their power to accomplish; but when you say "Well how, do you propose to do this?" they answer, "That's just it, I don't know," and often one finds them, after they have aimlessly drifted from pillar to post, and asks them "How did this happen?" "Why didn't you do differently?" they answer again in the same hopeless strain, "I didn't know."

The failure world is heaped high with those who "didn't know." They glut the marts of trades and professions, while there are positions calling insistently and constantly to those who do know, know that they know, and know how to express what they know.

Have a plan is the slogan of all success, from the worker who breaks rocks to the master The plan is the fulcrum which lifts the formless into form; until we have a plan of life, our world is void. We have to learn to say, "Let there be light" on our own pathway; and the plan is the ray of light that leads us into ultimate perfection.

Those who start their day without a plan are walking straight towards failure. I have seen women—housewives—begin their day without any plan. I have asked them, "What are you going to do today?" and they have answered, "Oh! I don't know, most anything," and their home has shown their violation of this basic law. It was a living lesson preaching its own sermon beside the home of the little conscious woman who said "Today, I shall do this and that or finish this, or that," who knew every step of her way, pushed all things into shape, and made a home out of the law, order and power of her own consciousness.

The first home is a failure home, the woman a failure as a home maker, a failure as a friend, wife, mother or anything she attempts, for a "I don't know" never produced anything but a family of "I don't knows," and "I don't know" is the corner stone of the home of despair and poverty.

There are places on the path where the human mind cannot include all the law of the past, present and future, but there is never a place where a mind worth calling a mind, cannot include control and command the now.

You can know what you want, how you want it, and what you are going to do about getting it, this hour, this day, and we know that whatever we put into time (today) we build into eternity (tomorrow).

If we hope for success we must become that success in our own mind, at once. We must build our plan as perfectly as an architect draws the pictured house, or the sculptor sets a sketch not first been projected in consciousness. Everything must live first in the brain of the master builder. It does not matter what the desire is, it must eventually come out into manifestation.

No matter what we want to do, we must work it all out in our mind just exactly as we want it to be. We must not allow our minds to accept one single idea that links us with less than the perfect. We must know what we want, how we want it and what we are going to do to get it, and then, every day be more and more insistent in our demand.

If you hope to go on from good, to better and best you only do so in the degree in which you bring the perfected vision of thought and action into unity.

Have a plan—then day and night live in the full realization of this plan—think, speak, be the thing itself. Do not accept anything than all desire; think it out to the smallest detail, for aimless drifting and formless drifting can take no part in the life of the one who would win.

Success by any other law than that of conscious, spiritual direction and control is built upon the law of change. If you drift accidentally into success you can accidentally drift out again, but the success gained through the law of self-knowledge and conscious obedience to God's Universal law of order, through the perfected spiritual arrangements and placing of our own human desires, is success forever, because it is the *at-one-ment* of human design with Universal intelligence.

"God helps those who help themselves" is a true axiom, and God the Universal Life, wants us to have everything that we want and will aid us to get it, as soon as we have intelligence enough to take universal direction.

When we, through higher understanding project the plan of our own human life and then resolutely command this plan to manifest, we will find that there is concerted action between the universal and personal laws of life and we can speak this plan into the very silences of the Universal Mind and myriad forms of success will come out and gather round us.

Holding the plan up before our own inner vision, projecting it into the very face of the Infinite All, following it with unclouded eyes unwaveringly as the sailor tracks the polar star, success of any or all kinds begins for us and can never end, for we have become the very law that we are seeking.

> *Let those who will, believe the old world law*
>   *That man was born to suffer length on length;*
> *It is a lie! The soul within us speaks.*
>   *We lift our thoughts and feel a new born strength.*

We are the lords of all our outer world;
We make the plan by which our life has might;
And as our thoughts of conquest forth are hurled,
We build the law of Peace, and Truth, and Right.

DON'T HURRY

When we have found our place in the great system of Universal Consciousness and have faithfully fulfilled all the personal side of the laws of adjustment; when our plan has become so crystallized that it hangs like a shining star of promise in our field of conscious thinking; when, sleeping or waking, we are one with the divine order of our desire, then we are really ready to receive fulfillment.

Why do we not receive it? There are many who have found themselves, built their plan with all the skill of a divine architect, yet the success that they seek eludes them. After days, nights, months, years perhaps, they sink down in despair saying, "There is no use trying."

I have a letter on my desk from someone telling the story of their struggle for success in the conquest of poverty; it says: "We have held on for years and done our best; but we don't seem to shove this bondage off of us. Jim is discouraged and has given up all hope of getting money enough to be free; somehow I haven't quit yet; I am still living in expectation. Can you help us to a fuller realization of our own power?"

This is the story of the multitude: "What is the next thing to do?" There is only one answer. Don't hurry—take your time live each day for all there is in it. There is not a step on the path that does not bring its own compensation. Twin born, the flowers of loss and gain bloom in full fragrance in time's paradise.

Life is a season; we are like a newborn plant and not all of life is born in us all at once. We ripen out of one law of consciousness and its embodiment, into others.

There are many desires, which take time to develop; they cannot come in a few days, hours or months.

If the thing you plan is a sublime and lasting thing to stand the test of time, it must draw inspiration from many moons of intensification.

> *"Grace is a moment's happy fortune,*
> *Power is a life's slow growth."*

We must remember that our today and our tomorrow of possession is linked with our yesterdays. We have often set many causes into operation in the past, which operates as a privilege or a lack of privilege in this new day.

There are lives that have many things to square with the Universal. Not everyone who says "Lord, Lord," will enter into the Kingdom of Health, Wealth, Love, Joy, Happiness or Freedom. "The Kingdom of Heaven (Harmony) is not taken by violence." We must reap what we have sown; reap all that stands between us and our new garnering, before the perfect fruit of all we desire will come to us. For the Law will take, and the Law will break, whatever is truly its own; and our delayed desires are but the signal of our own debts to the Universal Law of Love and Justice.

Many hearts throw down their hope at the very moment when they are just ready to receive life's gifts; they send them away by their changed consciousness; they do not know that substance is always changing, as is our position towards it, and that if we want to succeed we must keep the same hope eternally renewed under every and all setting. Time is an element in all human desires; time does not limit, it always fulfills, and waiting is one of the greatest human initiations.

After we have fully projected the plan, we have nothing to do but to water it continually with the rains, dews and showers of our expectations, and wait that hour when we have passed up the proofs of our own steadfastness. Some things by their own natural law will come slowly. "Soon the narcissus blooms and dies, but slow the flower whose blossoms are too mature to fruit." The life that can know itself and link up consciously with the Universal system of transference, by getting into its own natural groove, then steadily, unwaveringly, project its plan, and, flinging its whole conviction into it, wait patiently upon the law of the thing it desires, living in the consciousness of the eternal now, this life is one with the great Universal law of success; and as it sweeps on in rhythmic circles, it will come face to face with its desire, worked out in sane, sensible form.

On the fool's path are broken petals scattered,
  Telling of haste too eager to be blest;
While close beside, there shine the gleaming footprints,
  Were feet, too true for eagerness, have pressed.

CLEAN UP YOUR MOODS

We meet persons every day who have found themselves, who have a plan, who have patience to wait, and yet they are not a success. They find one engagement, one position, one home, one friend after another, but they are never happy, never satisfied, and change and confusion is over them.

What is the matter? Why are they not successful when they are filling so many of the success laws? This is the great question. Why?

Surely the reason is not very apparent, and one has to direct careful and deliberate attention to their life before the question can be answered for them. After enough thought and attention has been given, the reason pops up like a "jack-in the box" clamoring for recognition, and we are amazed that we did not know it sooner.

The answer is found in the unhappy disposition of the individual. Moods have wrecked tens of thousands.

"Clean up your moods!" This is the slogan of the successful person.

With a hateful disposition, no one can ever become a permanent success. Self-culture is not a myth. There are negative, destructive states of mind that will destroy the finest genius if they are allowed to manifest and take part in the individuality.

There are persons with dispositions so vicious that they are like biting dogs. No one is safe for a moment from the outbursts of their spiteful tongues and temper. Hasty temper has cost more than one person a good position; lost others a really valuable friend, and shut the door of grand opportunities.

No one wants as a friend, companion, wife, husband, employee or employer, one who is likely to fly off into a rage and lose his or her head at the slightest provocation.

Every condition worthwhile calls for poised, calm, self-controlled states of mind. In these there is power and opportunity; in haste and rage there is nothing but lack of opportunity and waste of energy.

I know a man, whose temper is like a raw-edged blade, continually cutting everyone who comes near it. He has his whole immediate family cowed down and afraid of him; everyone sidesteps his temper. He is allowed to go on each day, bullying the household into subjection.

Visiting there one day, the gentle mother, afraid of the effect some New Thought ideas might have upon this big tyrant, cautioned me, saying: "Now be careful, don't make Al mad." She said it for days, until at last I said: "Who is Al? He is no better than the rest of us, and why should I fear to make him mad? Let him get mad if he wants to. It is his privilege, but I am a free agent in consciousness, and the divine thinker of my own thoughts, and he had better look out that he does not make me mad."

No one had ever dared to "make him mad," yet the fact remained that he was "mad" all the time and a confirmed grouch.

The dear ones in the home, who love us, may protect us in our destructive states of consciousness, and we make them the victims of our moods and tenses; but there will come a time and place when the world will teach us that if we sulk or act spitefully we will do it alone.

The whole world of successful business waits for the big, genial, loving person, who will be a mascot for it; but it has no place for the crabbed, uncontrolled, moody, sulking individual, who thinks the whole world was made to serve and adjust to him or her.

We have no more right to pour our discordant states of mind into the lives of those around us, and rob them of their sunshine and brightness, than we have the right to enter their houses and steal the silverware.

Unhappy black moods, discouragement, hasty temper, sulks and grouches are mental habits, and they have no more right to be allowed to persist than any other indelicate, uncultivated habit.

It is just as uncouth to wear a sulk as it is to wear soiled clothing. Neither will be tolerated where the standards are true and high.

Gentleness, patience, consideration for others, self-forgetfulness and true selfness, are all the trophies of well-directed thought culture. They build up a personality that has one hundred per cent of attracting force.

We can be small, mean, narrow, bigoted and fault-finding, with our hand against all others and their hands against us, but as the years go by, we lose our value in every respect; our room is preferred to our company.

People will tolerate us, but they will not desire us, and after a while the whole world will pass us by, leaving us to eat out our hearts with the bitterness of spirit that our own discordant thinking has engendered within us.

We can set ourselves to clean up these endless little weaknesses of disposition, and put in their place, through persistent self-culture, the states of mind and heart which bring us forth as a personality valuable in every walk of life.

We can be "big," true and kind, patient, forbearing, full of wisdom and understanding, and the world will come and gather round us, no matter where our feet may wander, bringing us the fruits of our life's greatness. Success then is ours, to remain with us. Everyone seeks to receive something from and give something to the one who stands ever ready to give and receive.

Our personality and character becomes, then, our guarantee of ability; and the gentle attention, the sympathetic understanding, endears us to our friends and home, while our geniality, patience, forbearance and tranquility make us indispensable in the big discordant world of work and conquest.

MIND YOUR OWN BUSINESS

When we have found ourselves, made our plans, taken the attitude of active patience, cleaned up our moods, what is needed to precipitate into form our heart's desire? Many things; but chief among them all is the need of concentration; the power to know what we want, to know the way we want it, to be the divine thinker of our own thoughts; and, having done this, mind our own business.

This does not mean that we will be blind to other people's business, but that we will train our minds to be inclusive of all, but positive to outside desires.

"As ye did it unto the least of these, ye did it unto me," it is written in the New Testament, and a legitimate attention to everybody's wants, desires and purposes, is an important essential in the success of our own.

To be positive, however, in the thought of outside things, and negative to our own desires, is a failure law: any external thing that we endow with the power over us, will use this power simply because we have made it possible by our own thoughts.

The concentrated mind owns itself. It is success, and it thinks itself straight into the middle of the law of power. The diverse, flitting, rambling mind is a failure from the start, because the power of life lies in being able to unify all action, either mental or physical.

The ten thousand changes and conditions of life through which we are forced to pass in the search for what we call our success, demands that we arrange every step of the path of life with a precision and definiteness that is unimpeachable. "Our business" is our watchword, and our business is made up of every other people's business; but our business is the center around which our thoughts and actions must swing every waking hour.

No one else will or can mind our business but ourselves; the one who thinks differently is face to face that moment with failure.

We can so arrange our business that we mind it through a multitude of people who assist us, but these people are only a part of the plan of our business. They may assume complete control for that time and place, but if we drop them out of our consciousness, or worry about them, or break the law in any way, they will sometime become a rebellious factor and undermine our success.

Those who choose what they desire must stand by this desire and vitalize it into perfect success through their own thought force. If they leave it to become the caprice of other minds, or if they devitalize it by their concern about other businesses like their own, and put their thought into those things, thereby getting caught in the mesh of competition, they will fail in time.

They will not fail because their own business was not a winning thing, but because they took the lifeblood from it by their own foolish worry and resistance.

"Whatsoever thy hand findeth to do, do it with thy might," (Ecclesiates 10:10) is the keynote of success in any walk of life and the lodestone that will wrench from the Universal the things that we require.

A young physician, tired of the long hours of waiting for his practice, began to worry about the numerous calls and busy practices of his neighbor physicians, and after a while, to kill the monotony of the waiting he left his office and began to frequent a nearby club. An old friend, who had watched with concern the young doctor's career, finding his office empty day after day, printed this card, which he hung up in the doctor's office during one of the latter's visits to the club: "Keep your office and the office will keep you."

Mind your business. This was the true call to success for that life and he is now a successful surgeon with a large incorporated firm.

One time a friend gave me the address of a hairdresser, and needing her attention I took an opportunity to call upon her. As I came to the number on the street I found a large show window full of splendid hair, hair ornaments and figures with the latest modes of hairdressing, and I thought, "What a big splendid establishment this must be."

I went upstairs, took my place in the usual cabinet, and as the assistant was working on my hair, I heard a wonderful one-sided conversation over the telephone, between the owner of the establishment and one whom I judged to be the landlord, and I learned then and there that the window I had seen did not belong to the establishment. I found out in five minutes all about another firm, all its success, all its power to hurt this establishment, and that the landlord had let the lower floor to a competitive hair goods merchant, that the competitive hair goods merchant had done such a great week's trade, and that she had lost $200 from her usual week's returns.

I would never have known any of these things had the owner of the establishment that I was in minded her own business and held her tongue. She then and there spoke the other firm into success and herself into failure, and had she continued in that line of thought and action, she could have ruined herself by her own foolish methods, and she would have forever blamed it on the other hairdresser.

As I left, I said, "It is my privilege to teach you how to mind your own business. Will you come to my success lecture tomorrow night?"

She came; and I took this fundamental for the talk. She saw the law, and now has passed herself on into one success after another by refusing to endow any external thing with power over her own success law.

Mind your own business after you know what it is. No matter what anyone does or does not, it cannot affect you unless you think it can, and divert your power of creation and attraction by this thinking.

The law of divine attraction makes all of us one with *our* own, and *our* own is just what we create for ourselves; and nothing can take our own away.

We become the law of our own business, and it rises and falls at our own command and not from external command or competition.

Our business can only become a burning bush of power and attraction when we fan it into a white flame by the enthusiasm, attention and belief of our own life. From its own center must our own arise; the whole world's cinders cannot make it live or extinguish it.

In our own genius the germ of freedom, power and success lies, and day after day, with our eye single to our own business and double to the business of those around us, there will spring up for us such an eternal law of the action of finer forces that whatever our hand touches turns at once into that thing which we desire.

Our own business then, no matter what it is, objective or subjective, becomes a wonderful magnificent reality, which grows more and more brilliant as each day goes on and we intensify and re-intensify this great success law.

THE USE OF POWER

When we read the vast majority of books, with instruction of how to acquire success, we soon find that all their instructions are directed toward humankind in general and devoted to calling the attention of the unfortunate and unsuccessful to their faults; all efforts point to the reconstruction of the life of those who are down and out.

It seldom occurs to the ordinary mind that all things work together for the good or bad of everybody, and when the last word has been said to the employer, the employed, and the unemployed, there yet remain vast books to be written for the use of the employer, the leader, the controller of things and of people.

The employer, leader, or teacher and every life acting in a law of power and control has success and failure methods, and in the degree they operate them they take part in the up building or destruction of their own and others' success. "The one who teaches learns" and as soon as people are in a position of power where their advice is given and acted upon, they are linked eternally with those who act upon it—this is Karma, or the law of cause and effect, and through this they learn to give finer and finer advice.

There is a great cosmic law of "live and let live," and those who are the fittest in the struggle for existence have the strongest will to work either rightness or iniquity. Our place on the path determines our power and leaders, employers or managers who have the top round of the ladder of privilege and then deliberately kick the ones below them in the face, have the opportunity to do it, but not the right under the higher law of justice and they will do it at their own risk.

There are many people who remain obscure because they are unfit for authority, and there are brutal offensive lives everywhere in authority. Power gives the individual a chance to express his or her own real self and has little regard for the wants or feelings of others. Employers may bully their help along, they may sweat and drive them, getting the last cent's worth of labor out of them, and the employees may not be able to help themselves just at that moment, but the law of life keeps strict account, and somewhere the employers will feel the lash of their own law; sometimes the divine life current in the submerged employees will burst forth in mad rebellion or insurrection, then strife, and bloodshed will settle the case.

In Vancouver, British Columbia, I saw a sight that made me wonder "how long, oh, God, how long?" A great band of laborers, newly emigrated from India, were gathered together by a crowd of bosses to do some heavy labor. These people, some of them still wearing their native clothing, not one of them speaking a word of our language, knowing nothing at all of our world or its ways, and over them a big, brawling, ignorant boss, brutal, domineering, filled with the egoism of his own new authority; the workers were like dumb driven cattle, and there was no human hand or mind between them and their heartless master. It was his hour, but it was Truth's hour, too, and with every brutal curse and blow the cosmic hand wrote for him and moved on, and I read over his head: "God is not mocked, and what a man sows, that also shall he reap."

Again, in a restaurant, in Boston, a big blustering arrogant headwaiter, walking the floor in pompous authority spoke to every waitress as if she was his spaniel, instead of a hardworking human being. I heard what he said to the waitress at my table and I said to her, "Why do you allow such a bully to rule over you, why don't you hang up your apron and leave?"— She answered, "We have to take it because it is the same most everywhere, all waiters are at the mercy of a domineering headwaiter, and I have a mother to support and must keep my job, no matter how I am insulted."

A little learning, and a little power is a dangerous thing, and power misused can bring the longest round of despair. There are people in every walk of life, strong, positive, creative, able to cope with almost any condition, who never give a decent word or thought to those who are inferior to them, they are building their own failure law to meet them further on. They live in a world of inferiors, they never accept an equal or dream of a superior, and they poise themselves in an exalted spot and deal out their ultimatum to the rest of the world

Once a man came to me for success treatments. He said that he had always been successful, born so, had always had his own way, made money his will; he had been in a steady run of luck—health, success and power—until about a year ago, then things began to change. His success turned, investments failed, friends deceived him, and his help in factory and store were careless and impudent; his children had all gone abroad with their mother, he was alone, wondering why these things should come to him. I gave him the treatment but I knew that he was face to face with himself and I waited to show him a picture of himself before telling him the whole truth. The next day I called him on the phone. I purposely blundered my words, held him up, and called again. He roared over the phone, snapped, snarled, swore at the receptionist, gave a loud dictatorial order to some one while he was waiting to get my word. If I had opened the door of a bear pit I would have had as pleasant a greeting. I called him for two days repeating the experiment. When he came to our next meeting, I told him the story of the destructive use of power.

Forty years of cruel, hard, resistful compelling service; lack of appreciation, lack of patience, lack of tolerance—all had done their perfect failure work for him and failure was beginning to express its own law. His wife and children had left him, because, in spite of his name, place and power, he had sat at the head of his table cold—hard as flint; using his power to direct and control, but not to attract. His family had respected him, perhaps, had feared him, certainly, but loved him? Never—they could not, for he was everything but love.

Employers, and all who deal with the many, owe a great deal to the truth of harmonious association; those who are right with the lives that serve them will prosper; there are places when a big creative life cannot stand for suggestions from those who are not struggling, as they are, to pull off big things, and then they do not need to allow it. Take, for instance, an inventor sees his vision, and no one can expect to see it just as he does, and he has a right to be, to a marked degree, intolerant of others and their opinion, but to be so that no one can approach him and to be almost impossible to live with, so that all his assistants fear and despise him, this is not genius, it is pure uncontrolled moods and tenses, which, left to themselves, will destroy the very thing he desires. When we are really great in genius and understanding, we know that the biggest life is the one which includes the most, and who most perfectly expresses the things we do.

Those who have power to do, to say, to be, have also a great responsibility and as they act toward the very least of earth's children, they set the laws for themselves, in the long run. It has been written, "Ye shall not set your children's teeth on edge," and true leadership can only come to one who feels in all, and through all, the great law of justice and love.

"Do unto others as ye would that they should do unto you" is not too old to use in the New Civilization. Live for all you are worth yourself, but let the others have a chance to live too. This is true success; team work is hard to do perfectly, but if we use our genius, our power, our mastery to help others, and rise in deeper patience and helpfulness to the majesty of our place on the path, then power becomes a wonderful possession, our word never comes back to us void, and we can know that we are the highest expression of our own type of consciousness; that we can command, everything will love to obey, because we are one with all, in truth, in justice, and in power.

Seventh Success Method

FAITH

The polar opposite of faith is fear, and the great master and pioneer of mental science Helen Wilmans, wrote: "There is only one live devil, that is fear." And the more we study humanity and its many-sided expressions, the more we see the wisdom of her words. Fear, more than any other thing, operates against success. We can never reach the summit of our potential as long as we try to climb with this ball and chain weighing us down.

Fear stands as a gloomy sentinel and will not let the Spirit pass into possession of its best. The strands of failure are made from the fibers of fear; wherever fear is active, failure is its neighbor.

Looking at this very active agent we are obliged to ask the question, "where did fear originate, of what are we afraid, and why does fear dog the footsteps of the whole failure world?"

Try as we will to deny it, the fact remains that no matter how unfolded a human life is, there is always something of which it is afraid. Sometimes it is manifested as physical fear, sometimes as psychological fear, sometimes as spiritual fear, but fear of something and weakness of character in that partic-ular direction is a part of the scheme of the race unfoldment. And where fear is positive in the nature, controlling and limit-ing the life's natural forces, there is nothing on earth that will turn aside the negative results of this law.

Fear is the inheritance we have received from primeval times; the younger the nation, race or individual, the more fear there is expressed.

In the beginning of life, when humans first found them-selves, they found themselves surrounded by things with which they were totally unfamiliar. They found danger on every side; the roar of the wild beasts around them struck their souls and they soon found that they were in perpetual danger. In every unguarded moment they became prey for the beasts in the jungle. Hemmed in on every side by destroying elemental forces, they came by fear and caution to protect their own lives, Gradually this ever present need developed a fear consciousness which increased or decreased according to their power of coping with the elemental forces. Those who were able to outwit the beast, destroy the viper, escape the lightning stroke and withstand the wind and storms, gradually developed a moral courage which in time cast out all physical fear. These became the progenitors of all races of dauntless courage, but those who, slower in perception, cruder in action, and timid in power, grew more and more fearful, developed a fear consciousness that became the progenitor of a race of physical cowards. The descendants of these physical cowards are everywhere.

Ignorance and the lack of power was the root of the tree of fear. Its branches in the present day are self-consciousness and lack of true knowledge of self, people and condition.

We only fear what we do not understand. We fear physical conditions because they are unfamiliar with the things and conditions in them. We fear people because we do not know them.

Who ever thought of being afraid of one we loved? A perfect love casteth out all fear, and perfect love means perfect understanding. We will fear until we learn that there is nothing in the entire world of which we need to be afraid, and nothing can harm us but ourselves. The lion tamer has no fear of the den of lions, and Daniel in the lions' den was perfectly safe through this knowledge of the true laws of all life, his conscious union made for him a new condition.

We fear new conditions, because they are outside of our immediate experiences. There are some who would as soon face a loaded cannon as start in a new position, or meet a new responsibility, but after they are acquainted with it they are brave as a lion. All things are easy and commonplace as soon as they are old. There are crowds of failures simply because we are afraid of each other. Good actors and actresses have failed because they could not forget the crowd outside the footlights; fear brings self-consciousness, and this is death to all true greatness. Singers fail again and again because self-conscious fear stifles their breath and grips them so that they cannot express their best.

One season I had the opportunity of watching the workings of fear in the human mind. We gave weekly an afternoon New Thought matinee, and the first hour was devoted to reading, impersonations, and music, the other hour was given to the regular lecture. I heard many of the readers and singers at rehearsal with no one present but us. The singers sang like angels and did their parts in splendid power and abandon, but afterward, when the hour came for public work they failed to get themselves across the footlights or to be one-tenth of one per cent expressed! Why? They had a large, friendly, inspiring audience—people anxious and ready to be generous and accord them full recognition, but they failed to make a place for themselves in the heart of the public, because they were paralyzed with fear. They were afraid of their own kind; afraid of the civilized men and women who came out just to be entertained and who only asked of them that they should do their best. *Fear*, self-consciousness and lack of poise took away their immortal birthright and gave them a mess of pottage.

There is no cure for fear but faith. One has to first know the truth—that all life is the same life and everyone on the path of life is seeking the same things and going in the same direction. There is only one person on the path and that person is our self, yesterday, today or tomorrow. "No man is our friend or enemy, but all are our teachers."

There is no way of reducing life to a certainty. The years are always more or less full of things, people and conditions that are new. It is necessary for true progress, and to be afraid to meet each new day is soul cowardice, from which we must rescue ourselves. Life demands that we induce at a moment's notice an intelligence, which will cope with any and all things around us and do it masterfully. We, who have faith in ourselves will never doubt other things, we will build our resolve on this ideal and fling ourselves resolutely after it.

Over half of life is lived in consciousness, and idealization, and it takes a faith as boundless as our love of God to make it materialize. The substance of things hoped for are not easily transmuted into things gained and the only thing, which transmutes them, is *faith*. Through *faith*, Sarah conceived and bore Isaac, and through *faith* the most barren life can conceive ideals and holding fast to them, see them born into perfect manifestation. *Faith* makes the entrepreneur strong enough to venture and win. *Faith* teaches us to wait and trust until changing fortune again turns the wheel. *Faith* makes the friend, the lover, the mourner—all go forward with a hope that never fails. Fear has shut the door of success in the face of millions, but *faith* ever stands ready to open it and let the free spirit pass to new levels of peace, power and plenty. Success built upon faith is ever renewing. It remains because it is reborn over and over again through itself.

As Franklin D. Roosevelt told the American people, "All we have to fear is fear itself."

SELFNESS

When we have arrived at the eighth fundamental, we are beginning to have an intelligent idea of just what life requires of us, and our success or failure gathers around us according to the magnet we have made of ourselves.

One cannot go very far in self-analysis before finding out that all things gather round, leave and return to the self, and this self becomes an absorbing study.

There is no such thing in the world as unselfishness, if there were we would cease to exist, for the self is the center of the magnet called "the human being." It is the person him or herself and always will be. There are two distinct expressions of self—one of these makes for the eternal and abiding success and is drawn from the varieties of living; the other often brings an apparent success, but it is built on the laws of change which manifest eventually in failure. The success method is called by these—selfishness—but the new world calls one "selfness" or universality, and the other, separateness or personality. Upon these two great laws hang the past, present and future of every living soul.

Personality and universality are both states of consciousness and no one is to be blamed or praised because of them, but we must be taught of them, so that we will recognize the results of our own laws. The younger we are in the contact of the experiences of life, the more personal and separate we will be; we will only know ourselves and our own desires, our own aims and these will dominate our minds and actions. The everlasting ego stands out in pride and arrogance, and says to the whole world: "I—I want! I am! I must have," and I, me and mine is the trinity of our consciousness. On the path of life, in the association with others, we easily recognize this great army of egotists by their slogan, "what's in it for me?" This is their first and last word and unless there is something "in it" for them, they don't move.

Great wonderful things may be waiting everywhere, calling for a strong hand and a true heart to push them into form for the universal good, but their ears are deaf and their strength unattainable unless they can rise on these things of their own desires.

Personal egotists, separate, self-seeking often secures their own for a while, because they feed upon everything in their environment. They use everything as legitimate material to pave their way. They will rise to their immediate desire even if they step upon the heart of their best friends, and they often drags to slaughter the fondest love, which has laid itself at their feet.

It has been written in other words by those who knew, "The wicked flourish like the green bay tree," but it is also written, "Leave them alone, they be blind leaders of the blind, and if the blind lead the blind, they both will fall into the ditch and life, everywhere, proves that this is true. They may have and hold till the want grows cold whatever is their desire, and may squeeze out of it all that is in it for them, but they are one with the law of their own relationship, and this is change. The universal law of life is on their trail, and it is the law of God that the consciousness and things of "I, me and mine," must pass on, and through the experiences that come to them through these desires they can and will go on with the higher law of "ours," and still farther into the true selfness, and universality of thine.

The failures come to the personal life because in its own conceited selfhood it links itself with the method that brings failure. We must eventually lose our opportunities when everyone knows that we operate every action of our life by what we will get out of it. Employees will leave a firm some day where only the employers' interests are served; the hour may be long delayed because of the lack of true selfness of the employees but the handwriting is on the wall and they must meet their own method. Employees who show that their whole interest is personal and who work only for what there is in it for them are failures. There are thousands of such failures. Why? Because in their search for opportunities and work they were not really hunting these, but were really hunting a nice soft snap, where they could draw a good salary and get all out of it they can and give nothing in return; they want to get three hours' pay for one hour's work; their employers soon discover it and above their exalted ego write the word "shirk."

We get out of life what we put in it and the balance of success turns on the law of "with what measure ye mete, it shall be meted unto you." The personal, separate life loses its value as a friend and in time finds itself forgotten and counted out, for tolerance ceases to be a virtue when it forces friendship into personal service. These people fail just as surely in love. True it is that "love suffereth long and is kind, does not take offense, seeks to give of itself," but love must love, and after a while it will turn away just as naturally as the sunflower turns to the sun, and claim its own where it finds it.

A sweet, true patient love is something to give and gain, but it is not worth the price of a soul paid down. Unless one gets a soul in exchange he or she will some day take it out of the grasp of the tyrant who is using it and put it back into the Divine life, to await the perfect answer to its call. Robbed at last of opportunities, privileges, friends, and love, "every tree that the Heavenly Father hath not planted is rooted up" and standing with the wreckage of their own storm around them, they are forced into the ditch and in failure and despair are ready to eat the crumbs that fall from the universal table. Here we find them and knowing the law we give them the key to their own self-made condition and regeneration can begin. The law of selfness saves them and they come out into success and power: Stronger often, and more steadfast than those who have not paid so great a price for the higher knowing.

No one lives to oneself alone and no one dieth only to oneself! This is the great law of universality, selfness and success. The sooner we know this and merge our own life into the manifold interests of others, the more quickly our own desires will be manifested and things born of this law are ours forever. The personal success that comes to us through universal association with interest and helpfulness to others is a verity that time will only make more truly our own.

We cannot push our personal desires through the very center of another's hopes and find lasting success. We cannot fling down the aspiration and dreams of another and climb by them into eternal fame and glory. We cannot step over a broken human heart to continuous happiness; the law of life is not mocked, but we can link our life, our dreams, our aspirations, our love with the deep centralized desires of those around us and mount as by eagles' wings to the very mountain tops of our hearts' desires. We are only atoms in the whole, and in the long run, all love is blessed by love, all helpfulness-by-helpfulness, all service-by-service.

All small lives talk, live and act separateness, egoism and personalities, and they will by natural law register these things around them in failure until they learn through failure the weakness of their law.

All great lives talk, live and act principles of unity, love, understanding and service. This makes them one with the truth of life in the highest and around them must come an ever-increasing success power.

YESTERDAY, TODAY AND TOMORROW

There are few things about which the world is so genuinely stupid as the true attitude to yesterday, today and tomorrow.

The obsession of this trinity of time, stands as a sentinel and will not let the race mind pass into a peaceful mental or spiritual state.

Remorse about yesterday, uncertainty about today and dread of tomorrow drives the human consciousness on into a wild burst of psychical despair from which only the strong word of truth will ever rescue it.

There are thousands of failure lives caught in the destructive obsession of yesterday; they have tried and failed; their past is full of regret, remorse and rebellion against conditions over which they apparently have no control; fortunes lost, friends gone, opportunities passed by, old age with them, they sink down in weakened courage and go round and round in the thought dragnet of their dead yesterdays, they think of all they have not succeeded in accomplishing, think of deeds done which had better have been left undone. All these take the light from the eye, the spring from the step, the courage from their hearts, and there is no possibility of their accrediting themselves in a new way for they are one with the deepest degree of failure, and they never know that they are building it for themselves.

Regret, remorse and bitter, jealous memories are devils born of ignorance and strife; when these, united through the soul, come thronging, the gates of hell swing inward for that life, and only that person can close them; and can close them with no uncertain hand when it is understood that the past, present and future are one. There is no such thing as a mistake; no such thing as lost opportunities; there is no such thing as the past there is just life, and more and more life. Everything is the Eternal now, and every hour behind us on the path was that this hour might be, and our experiences of yesterday were simply the methods which life took to drive us on into higher things.

People always do exactly the best they know how to do, they often think that they did not do the best, but the fact remains that their actions are always based on their own consciousness, and somewhere in their own mind certain laws obtained which made it impossible for them to do differently just at that time. Perhaps they might have done differently had they known five minutes before what they knew five minutes after the doing, but this wisdom came as the result of doing. "Experience is a dear teacher, but fools won't learn any other way."

Since we know that life is for experience, expression and inclusion, we stop our failure method—we do not look back—we keep out of the past. It has no message that we can understand, save what it speaks to us In the today must come out in our today, and if we are continually recreating our old hours with our thoughts of today, we will never get free. If we want to go on to the new success awaiting us we must unwrap ourselves from the grave clothes of our yesterday.

There is no use grieving over anything; no use recalling a painful memory. Let it go! Life is always a going on; Our faces were set to go forward, walking backward we stumble. And there are always big new things ahead if we keep after them.

One continuing and persistent obsession is the one of old age. "If I were young" has stood in the way of multitudes. This certainly is a young people's age, and the really old man or woman has little hope of success as long as he or she holds on to old age. But in truth there is no *old* age, there is *age*; youth and age have no relationship to each other, and each has its own laws of success and conquest. Only the persons who allow themselves to really be old in their age will ever be a failure. Old age is waning enthusiasm. As long as we keep enthusiasm and interest and unity we will find our place waiting for us. True it will not be among those of youth, nor in the occupations of youth, but age has its demands which youth can no more fill than age can fill youth's position.

There are thousands of places, positions and conditions of life that call for the poise and judgment of mature minds, and the person with age and wisdom can fill these places.

It was written that after many serious accidents on a certain railroad a close investigation showed that they occurred through employees not remembering orders; through some one being asleep at the post, and another too late to receive a message when he should have been there, and the final decision was, "the workers are too young." It could easily be seen that in such important places the sober judgment, lasting strength and physical endurance of older people were demanded. Youth has dash and glow and power to rush ahead and pioneer, but age has grit, endurance, steadfastness and power to hold on through hours of suspense and supreme tests, and these two avenues of life must forever be filled. Those who are obsessed with the thought of old age are shutting their own door of opportunity and no one says no to them but themselves.

Once I was asked, "what is there in life or a woman after she is fifty?" The old world says, "nothing," the only thing that she can do is to bury herself, and the old world said also "men after forty should be chloroformed." We have quit letting the croaker, the pessimist and the fatalist think and speak for the world. At fifty a man or woman is just beginning real life; they have finished their processes and are ready to begin a real existence; they have in them the wisdom born of many experiences, and their life can become a veritable cedar of Lebanon sheltering many tribes.

If they seek the things in life, the people or the opportunities where age is a valuable factor, they will be one with a success higher than they have ever conceived existed for them. With experience, poise, power, endurance and a young heart, and a clear mind that understands life and its needs, age is a royal pathway of power and wisdom and the young everywhere will come and gather around and bring the fruit of their lives' greatness.

We can be old in heart, mind, body, crabbed, set apart and morbid over our increasing years and waning opportunities, and the world will pass us by, letting us die alone.

The obsession of today is another great stumbling block. There are thousands who expect to take out of today all their hopes and dreams, and weep because the day passes and nothing comes to them, they do not know that they are the cause of their own delay. Today is the product of our yesterday, and it is given us so that we may each day plus our own consciousness.

We can never take out of today anything that we did not create for ourselves in our yesterday. Time and eternity are one. What we build into today passes with us into our tomorrow, and when we face days and days of emptiness, it is a certain fact that in all our yesterdays, we did not accomplish the law of our desires. If we want to meet a day full of joy, love, peace and opportunity, we must live these things every passing hour, holding fast to them in faith. Then as time passes by, our days plus each other and in some unexpected day we will meet all our own power and a perfect day that will continue according to the power that has been generated.

No one is to blame but ourselves if our today narrows down to dull, dreary monotony, and our life to petty confines; we reap what we sow, and we can never reap the harvest of anything unless we have sown the seed somewhere; nothing and nothing make nothing, and the way to get something into expression for ourselves is to set about creating it for ourselves in each hour of living; we can always live unfalteringly in the ultimate until it comes.

"Where now we wait a dreary waste may be,
With no green thing to glad our longing eyes
And far away across the bounding seas
Are bid the balmy isles of Paradise."

If we begin to fill our today with true understanding everything will change for us. There are many portals to Paradise, and we can open one for ourselves any moment by beginning to live in consciousness the law of that which we call "Paradise."

Standing fast, then, we can call, and it must come, not by living months and years of waiting, but now, for in full realization, a thousand years are as but as one day!

The *obsession of tomorrow* is always recognized just as easily as one detects the traces of yesterday and today. The obsession spreads out all over those who are caught in its negative dragnet.

"Going to do it"—this is their slogan. "Going to have it"—"Some day." The future, like a mighty ruler, stands before them and worshipping it they are blind, deaf and dumb to their present opportunities.

There are wondrous avenues of accomplishment opening on every hand, but something in their weak consciousness says, "wait" "not now" "some other time." "Going to do it" is the finished law of procrastination. Procrastination is the seed, and "going to do it" the tree that springs from the obsession. There is nothing in this world that ever springs spontaneously perfect. Creation, emanation and evolution are cosmic laws, and they are human laws too. And no matter what we want, have, do or be, we must begin it before we can finish it and possess the fruition. Those who carry hope, dreams, and desires hidden in their hearts, and drag through days, months and years without the courage of putting it to the test, must be a failure because they are standing ever before their own unfulfilled selfhood. "God helps those who help themselves" has been spoken for centuries, and a thousand unseen forces are waiting to assist those who know what they want and then fling themselves fearlessly in pursuit of their goals.

Once I met a great woman, great in genius, great in personality, great in expression. She was training to become a public reader and teacher and perhaps later an actress. In some past incarnations she had fulfilled the law of all these desires and into life equipped fully for these big endeavors. I was fond of her and eager for the world to have the privilege of enjoying her great gifts. Always she said, "Not yet, but I am going to do it." Then she went on studying, always with this discordant urge within her, she longed to stop and get out into her legitimate field. Whenever she came to me, I said, "why don't you begin, get ready, announce yourself, get a business manager or get into a company, won't you please do something to give yourself a chance?" Yes, she would, she was "going to do it." Ten years have passed and she has never done it and today, after ten years of foolish resistance and wear and tear on the physical side which repressed genius always brings, she is the decay of a glorious selfhood; lacking that subtle essence of divine command within her own soul. She lost all, and will have to give this incarnation to the development of a consciousness that can direct her own soul. The world is full of those who are "going to do it" and so it is full of failures.

"Do it now," is the watchword of success. It is common sense to give ourselves a legitimate amount of time to get ready for anything. The bigger our endeavor, the more time and thought it demands, and it is well said, "fools rush in where angels fear to tread," but it is also true that without this quality in the human soul which causes the fool to rush in, there are many fools who would forever remain at the fool's level of unfoldment. The urge that sends the fool on is the urge that deifies and glorifies our human endeavor and the fool follows it in uncontrolled, undirected enthusiasm, while wise people guides it, cherishes it as their most precious possession, training themselves to allow it to urge them on and through almost impossible accomplishments.

"Going to do it" never gets anyone anywhere, and those who rise powerfully to the top of their own mountain of success, are those who first survey the path to this mountain pass and then taking the bit of the bridle of their own lives in their teeth, race to success.

It is then that the world seeing them rush on in what appears to be madness stops and asks, "What is this?" And with attention comes interest, and through interest comes praise or ridicule, and through these comes co-operation and success is assured. Finding ourselves, knowing what we want to do, giving ourselves a legitimate time for perfecting our ability to do, then *doing* it this is *the law of success.*

Do it now! We may have only one-tenth of one per cent perfection when we start anything, but practice makes perfect, and out of the very crudest material will come a gem, polished by use into a resplendent brightness. It is better to do and fail and profit by the wisdom born of this failure, than to sit down in unexpressed genius and atrophy from disuse. "The past is spent, the future is thy God's, today is thine, hold fast the precious treasure."

PSYCHOLOGICAL SINS

The world is full of psychological sins. Every hour some one is transgressing the higher laws of truth, trampling down that which is fine and right and putting in its place the imperfect, the crude; defeating one's own purpose through the blindness of one's own consciousness. The old world has said, "life is just the difference between *Tweedlededum*, arid *tweedledee*, but the *Tweedledees* have it" and this means that those who consciously or otherwise contact and express at all times the true law of a condition, time, place or person, have gained a power unknown and unpossessed by the blundering multitude who never see into the real center of things. Psychological sins are the little foxes in the vines of success that eat out for many the very roots of life.

To be able to always say, do and be the right thing at the right time, demands a high degree of consciousness, but in the measure that we pass up the proofs of such a law there hangs our own personal privileges and opportunities for progress.

The names of psychological sins are legion, and each of us has our own particular form of sinning, and it often demands microscopic spiritual examination to find the spot through which the law is operated.

There are many avocations in which one fails again and again and still goes on working through into a bigger possibility; the law of life forgives our transgressions, and as we remit our own sins they are remitted for us, But those who watch the race progress, know that the one who persistently is guilty of psychological sins will never be forgiven, neither in this world, nor in the world to come as long as this violation of psychology continues.

Chief among all psychological breaks, a prime factor in the production of failure, is the lack of sense that will tell you when to hold your tongue. Talk has beggared thousands. No matter how carefully it is used, it is bound to come that some day one will talk too much to the wrong person. It is not so much the sin of not minding your own business, as it is the love of talking.

There are always many things that others need not know; it is a violation of all true being to talk about these things. To hold our tongues about our own affairs and the affairs of others especially—this is power. We may tell our secrets to the idle listener if we choose, we only hurt ourselves thereby, but what we think about some one else, and pour out with our own senseless talk is double sinning and seldom one cares to hear it and we become a bore to be avoided. Again, there are those who say, "you can believe that I always say what I think and if I think anything, I am going to say it." Wrong again! No real psychologists ever says just what they think unless their finer senses tip them off that that is just the moment to say that very thing. There is a time for everything and nothing in all God's universe but our own ignorance ever gave us the commandment to go around spilling our "says" out uninvited. In fact, what we say often cuts no figure with the real truth. Our "think" and "say" are good for us to act by, but they might be entirely incorrect in analysis and the direction of others. It takes years of experiences and fine discrimination before the things that we say will not come back to us void, and we only get ourselves disliked and delay our own law of larger usefulness by meddling.

Another sin is to play the traitor in small hidden ways to friendship, business or love of others, a trifling betrayal of weak spots in their character or work or business, which they, unconsciously, put in our hands, or which we arrived at through the intimacy of friendship, and a friendship which made it appear possible for them to live for a moment, perhaps, off their guard. Every human life is transmuting something either in the self or environment. The guise of friendship allows a closer intimacy than is accorded to others, and through this we enter into shrines and temples of lives, which are kept, closed and sealed to the big useless crowd outside. It is a sin of the deepest dye not to have a shrine of absolute truth in our own life, and then to sneak like a thief in the night into the holy sacredness of another's shrine and turn from this to the outside world, tear down this shrine and demolish this temple with insidious hints and half-veiled suggestions until we have let loose a floodtide of suspicion around it. This is *theft* on the subjective side of life, and as nature avenges herself on the material thief, just so the Higher Avenger of truth takes strict account. Even Hell itself has no respect for its own valiants!

On the path of life these human weeds flourish for a time, "suffering no flower, except their own, to rise," and often it seems as if the flower of their ultimate failure was slow to ripen, but the mills of the gods grinding slowly are daily bringing them nearer and nearer their own law. We may never be able to fix the truth upon them; they are never found out, but the "hound of Heaven" tracks them down. We meet them everywhere. They hear the baying of the hound in their woods, and weighted down by disease, loss and poverty, often despair; they ask the reason of their failure, and then it is that New Thought gives them a pen or word picture of themselves.

Amid all the great psychological sins, there are thousands of minor ones: lack of attention, lack of earnestness; lack of reverence for truly holy things; taking one's self too seriously; failing to give a legitimate interest to other people's problems; untidiness; vulgarity; unnecessary mannerisms which we would be better without; quick offense to a well-deserved correction or suggestion; white lies; procrastination; continuous evasions; pretensions—all of these eventually crystallize into some big failure law of character and consciousness.

Psychological sins are the streams that are converging to make the river of a consciousness in which float liars, thieves and criminals—these are only the finished product of the negative psychological law.

Success is the product of psychological righteousness or rightness. Honor, integrity, truth, faithfulness, and steadfastness—all these link us with a cosmic current of power that will manifest for us anything we declare.

Those who would lose their right hand rather than betray a friend will never lack friends, and they will be for them the ladder of success up which they will climb to their own perfect accomplishment.

Those who can be taught and who will find in everyone and take from everyone a lesson, will soon learn that they have included enough wisdom to be teachers themselves and that the whole world is wearing out their doorsills.

Those who will stand on silent guard until death, if need be, before the shrines and temples of those who have allowed them to enter, will find their own shrines glow with a new radiance, for "no greater love hath any man than this, that he lay down his life for his friend."

When we have tracked down and killed all the little psychological foxes in our vines of success, we will soon find them bursting forth with strength and fruitfulness, and success will be our eternal possession because we harvest it from our own fields.

BUSINESS, BUT NOT TRUTH

Nothing but truth will hold truth, and failure comes as the inevitable reaction of being continually just off the center of absolute truth.

If we continuously link ourselves with things that are just a little off color, we will find our law returning to us some day in the form of a liar, a thief, or some other equally destructive expression. These lies may be so close to truth that the ordinary individual never detects them, but they are lies just the same and their father is lies, and their mother is destruction.

In the business world we meet these failure methods everywhere; salespeople will sell you goods they know are being misrepresented, but they aim only to make sales regardless of everything and it is called good business. It may be good business but not truth, and after a while you meet them and they are struggling with big business reverses and they wonder how the cyclone of reversals hit them. They forget, or never stopped to think of, the failure law they daily intensified.

A saleswoman who was truth first and business second, went to clerk for a business firm. The first thing the proprietor taught her was how to operate the law of business lies. He said: "There is a drawer full of pins, they are all cheap pins, and cost one cent a paper. When a customer comes in, ask her if she wants a five or ten cent paper of pins, and no matter which she says take them from this drawer." Again he said: "A great many drinking men come in here. You are a charming woman. Whenever a man is a little tipsy, jolly him along and get all of his money; a drunken man always spends and a clever woman like you ought never to let a man get out with a cent in his pocket."

This woman was a good saleswoman and worked faithfully for a week under her employer's law of business, not truth. She saw hourly, how, himself, his using their own true success law to the destructive power of eventual failure, and although she needed money to support herself and her child, she went to this man and said, "I refuse to sell my own soul for a mess of pottage; when I sell ten cent pins they shall represent that value, and when I sell to men they shall have their senses undrugged by dope or liquor." As this employer gave her her wages, he said, "I am glad to get rid of you, with such talk you would kill my business." Two years from that day the firm was in bankruptcy, and the saleswoman secure in a permanent position with a reliable house.

Business, but not truth, brings its own adjustment; the law of justice is after all "an eye for an eye, and a tooth for a tooth." There are dentists who fail because over a long period of time they willfully misrepresent prices and work. It may be easy to deceive a naïve or uneducated person, and it is easy to ask double the price because a doctor's patient calls in a limousine and has money. As the customer or patient cannot find out the real value; you are in a seat of power and business is business, but unseen fate watches and the universe takes strict account, and it is the universe which collects the balance of lies and false business.

Many M.D.'s have found, after years of practice, that they were stranded high and dry without patients, reduced from a lucrative practice to nothing! "Why," they ask, "once I did a good business!" Nine times out of ten the answer is written—"Business, but not Truth!" It was easy to keep a patient under the idea that he or she was ill for months after that person recovered, because it produced a good fee and the person could afford it. It is easy to ask an exorbitant fee for a simple operation because the patient must have the operation, and it is so easy when one is in the seat of power to misuse that power. And so this misuse goes on until it falls back into form, and the one who fulfills the laws must be carried along in its currents.

All these lies or these actions just off the line of truth, will gather as a boomerang and as time goes on they must come back to where they started.

The whole industrial, professional, political, and social world is filled with these violations of truth, and in business partnership, homes, marriage, and love, everywhere, they are rampant and yet the poor struggling people ask why are there so many failures?

Perhaps in no association are there quite so many false positions intensified as in what the world calls love. The world will say it truly loves and then lie with the next breath. A husband writes: "I am so glad, dear, you are having a good time while you are away" which is pure sarcasm as he is sick with jealous pain because "dear" is away alone.

A woman says: "I love him with all my heart, but I pretend I don't; it wouldn't do to let him know it, he would be so domineering." Yet they call this love, when, in truth, love only loves, it never domineers, and true love is always glad, it is never jealous or unhappy; there cannot be any permanent success for such association, and it is this which has led the world to say marriage and love are a failure; such marriages and such loves are failures because they are one with failure methods. But true marriages and true love are life's holiest success, because they are built upon the law of true understanding and not pretension.

The highest and greatest permanent successes are built around the lives of those who stand steadfast for truth, the whole truth and nothing but the truth.

Whoever wants business success, love or ambition to blossom into fruition, must have the absolute principle of truth in his heart. It is said that civilization today does not permit truth to be either spoken or lived—this is the *master lie*, hatched in the consciousness of the prince of liars, and sent forth by those who are living the life of business but not truth. It fits their development to say this and if possible hold the mass mind to their own levels.

There are in all this seething mass of misdirected energy seeds of mighty truth, and a new civilization is rising which speaks the truth and whose business, love, home and social relationships are assuming new and beautiful expressions.

We know today that the straight road of truth, through the jungle of the old civilization, is a hard climb, and truth is beset on every hand with opportunity to change horses with liars, but the quickest way to our perfect success, no matter what it is that we desire, is to live each hour in unfaltering steadfastness to the truths of life.

It is true that truth takes the long road and that sometimes the hour seems long delayed, but it is also true that when this law accomplishes our ideals, they are verities and the true commercial world is waiting to pay us a big price for our verity. The world of friendship is waiting to worship at our feet, for truth has reached the heart of truth, and faith knows that it can work out its own through this rock of support beneath it.

Failure must forever be the inheritance of the liar:, but success in the highest comes some day to the life which is true to God, true to itself, true to its work, true to its own ideal. The world really loves truth; it loves the one who can fearlessly tell the truth, and it is waiting for that master-consciousness who can tell the truth about all things in a way which will not offend.

PERSONALITY AND INDIVIDUALITY

There is a great place for higher instruction in the subject of personality and individuality, and one of the greatest blunders of age comes in directing the mind into a line of thinking which separates these two distinct expressions of the self; they are both important, and only as we understand them can we harmonize them for power, and when we do harmonize them, the world witnesses a gigantic success law which makes all other laws look puny and insignificant, then it seems as if all laws were finished in this perfect magnet called the human being.

Humankind is the visible and audible expression of spirit, the energy which comes from this expression is the unseen energy of life. It is spirit itself. The energy of every life is the unseen side of that life, just as the unseen energy of a rose is shown forth in the perfume, and the energy of light is thrown out as heat. This energy of life is subject to control just as heat is controlled.

The external body, that which we see and touch, is simply thought energy materialized; we have been taught to call this "personality." Personality is really only that energy which we have thought into expression and it bears witness to our own estimate of ourselves. Our body or personality becomes the expression of just what we have created in the infinite energy and localized on the objective plane for our use.

One sees the personality, but only feels the individuality; it is the subtle something which radiates from us. One may possess a very displeasing personality and yet radiate a very pleasing individuality. There are personalities, which are really repellent, but often after we know them we find a wonderful individuality hidden within them, and are charmed with it and so learn to forget the displeasing exterior.

Individuality is the positive pole of being and thinking, and our personality is the negative pole. The one who has a displeasing personality and a pleasing individuality, tells every passer-by that he or she has succumbed to negative inharmonious lines of thinking, if not here then in some other state of consciousness, and that he or she has lived in the external mind and has been caught in the diverse currents, and the laws, of common consciousness, and that in this life has not yet learned to join the two forces. Often we have heard people say, "Sally is a grand individual and her personality is in keeping with her character." This means that the same quality runs through and through Sally, that the warp is the same as the pattern.

Our personality will naturally put on a different expression from the individuality when, by force of habit, either inborn or acquired, we make our consciousness dependent on external things, instead of controlling and directing all external conditions by the law of life from within.

Individuality is an expression of conscious growth and our personality may be made the perfect objective expression of this growth.

The purely personal life is not a whole life at all; it is only a part, just as the body is only a part of the divine person. Individuality is often latent in every life and after the development of the personality is over, the individuality begins to speak forth; it is nothing but the finer thought life that has been growing throughout all time.

Every moment of our life individuality is adding to itself and personality is adding to itself and when the two become one, the same material is used for both and there is no longer need for transmutation. But as long as there is separation between them, one may know that there is some work yet to do in life. The whole scheme of existence makes for absorption of the lesser into the greater, the subliming of all matter into the manifestation of spirit.

The law of each life demands that the personality and individuality become joined so that the individuality may express externally as well as internally, that is, to become the visible as well as the invisible power. The personal must become refined and etherialized through the stimulation of the higher impulses.

The personality is the workshop and our thoughts are the tools with which the tireless sculptor cuts away all gross material until the very image of the divine soul within stands revealed in the personality of flesh and blood and sinew.

We all know just how many beautiful thoughts we have (which often fail to materialize) because we do not believe them to be true. These thoughts are all creative ones and are generated in the individuality, which is often telling us what splendid radiant creatures we are, or may become, and how often we submit these imaginings to our personal mind and are told that they are too fantastic to clothe with form; we accept the verdict of our common consciousness and build our personality with the idea of something less than perfection, when the very soul within us is screaming out the message that we may become divine if we so desire. Our common consciousness is comrade to our personality and through it we become children of the earth; our individuality is comrade with our illumined supra-consciousness, and through it we know we are the children of the Most High.

The better we understand our life in the individuality side, the more perfect the personal expression becomes and the farther we advance away from the limitations; it is then we turn perception into the freedom of revelation.

Every positive creative thought is added to the individuality and each day developing a higher function of the body. Every thought we carry is creative and must by natural law express somewhere; it must be localized in the physical body or it must be represented as energy, which we radiate through the body. The more crude the thought generated, the denser must the body and the radiations become. The personality and individuality never were and never can be anything else than the negative and positive reaction of the same power and this power, Infinite consciousness, expressed here in human form.

Individuality will forever remain the twin of personality until humankind merges them together; they were born together and they will remain together until the higher absorbs and controls the lesser.

The visible world and the visible body are both under the same law. The external grows from a fuller rushing out of the inner life; the personalities grow and refine through the new truths learned; the closer it allows itself to follow the invisible but insistent individuality, the more beautiful and harmonious it becomes.

In the struggle for existence and the accomplishment of our success law, both personality and individuality have their power, and those who forget, find it out later on to their sorrow. Our personality is our introduction to the world, it is the real press agent to the multitude, and it speaks a silent message and depends wholly upon us to make it tell a wonderfully attractive message. No matter how beautiful we may be in mind and character we are just that much more attractive if we have all this joined and expressed in our personality. No matter how unattractive anyone may be there is always one personal charm that can be made the center around which individuality can attract and manifest. If we neglect to find our strong personal point of power and intensify it, we do so at our own risk. Sometimes this point of beauty or attraction is only nice hair, it might be luminous eyes, perhaps a gentle smile or a tranquil expression, possibly good teeth, aristocratic feet, a supple figure, a splendid walk, broad shoulders, a cheery laugh—each one of these makes a fulcrum of power for the one who will use them and not go moping around because she or he does not have them all.

Business, more than anything else, calls for power personalities; personalities that have strong marked characteristics on which faith can be established. This will lead the seeking world on into *at-one-ment* with the individuality. I have often heard business executives say, "Oh, I can't send Frank, he hasn't personality enough, and can't use what he has." All public opportunities and privileges call for personalities to fit them. All great movements on any plane demand personalities to stamp them into the minds of the race. The heads of the Roman Church who went to hear and see Martin Luther when he was pioneering his new religious idea to the world, said: "Pshaw! That man hasn't a thing on earth but a personality!" But that personality burnt the message eternal into race consciousness.

The very acme of success depends on our having one hundred per cent of our personality expressed all the time, and one of the sure failure paths of life is to allow our personality to become so demagnetized that it has in it no hint of the true self. The world may say, "Anna is just as beautiful as she can be, but, poor thing, she cannot be very beautiful," and this may be true, but if we make ourselves just as beautiful strong, sweet, kind, neat, and wholesome as we can, then we have fulfilled the true law of our own being and can laugh the whole world in the face. As we become more and more perfect in the transmutation and reformation of our personality, this fineness sinks in and stays in our consciousness and joins our individuality, and our individuality each day grows more wonderful, and this perfecting individuality plays all its strong impulses out through our face and form, and we again return them still finer through action and understanding, until our psychic circle of power is complete, then we become a magnet of attraction and in every walk of life there radiates from us a great love, power, success and liveliness, and our very presence becomes a benediction. We are not then seeking success, we *are* success and the whole world pays tribute to our individualized personality.

ENTHUSIASM

There is nothing in all the world but life! Even Death itself is only life acting inversely.

One of the greatest success methods is to be full of a radiant energy. We are judged every moment by the law of whether we are "the quick or the dead." There are multitudes of dead ones everywhere, and these make the vast army in failure. You may go among the poverty-stricken, the unemployed or the loafing world, and you will find that the quickness of spirit is lacking in them; they are dead to opportunities; dead to enthusiasm; dead to faith; dead in vital understanding and dead to everything that will hold them fast to the great pulsing life current, everywhere waiting their own conscious contact. These failure people are depressed below the level of the universal life, like the Dead Sea, or the parched sands of the desert, while within their own being are lying dormant, the possibilities of life more abundant and the success that comes from this life.

There are those everywhere who take nothing out of life and who put nothing into it; if it were not that the Heavenly Father feedeth them they would perish off the earth. There are many people who live in all the beauty of this earth, contacting hourly the wonders of earth, sky, sun, water, and verdure, and yet are blind and deaf to all that nature's voice is speaking. "The great wide, beautiful world, with the wonderful waters around it curled, and the wonderful grasses on its breast," are nothing at all to the lives and eyes of the dead ones—they have no value as friends, companions or lovers, for all these associations call for the thrill of the quickening power of sight and sense, to make them worth while. They have no real value anywhere and are a drag on every situation because they have within them no power of response to any sort of external stimulation. They lack the power to press their own spring of answering enthusiasm and quickness.

Enthusiasm is the dynamics of our personality. Without it, whatever abilities you may possess lie dormant. It is safe to say that all of us have more latent power than we ever learn to use. We may have knowledge, sound judgment, and good reasoning facilities. But no one, not even ourselves, will know it until we learn how to put our hearts into thought and action.

In the commercial world deadness makes them ciphers in the big active sum valuations. One day in a New York subway station I saw a shoe shining stand. It was splendidly appointed with cabinets and chairs; there was a bootblack at each chair. As I passed I saw one of these bootblacks, with bright eyes, standing alert beside his particular booth and with a cheery ringing voice he called to every passer-by, "Shine, shine, shine 'em up, have a shine, Sir?" Everybody's attention was arrested, busy men looked down at their shoes, and one immediately sat down while three others waited their turn. The other bootblack was asleep at the corner of his booth, indolent, lazy, uninterested in life, in the crowd, or even in his own business; his drooping figure, his carelessness, the drowsy snore, all told their own story, yet the world would have blamed his brutal boss could they have seen him kick the bootblack into wakefulness. To sleep at such a time and in such a place was negative energy enough to link him with the law of kicks both human and divine. I looked at the picture—one all life and power, the perfect picture of true success and then at the other, the perfect picture of failure and my heart said, "The quick or the dead," and I knew again what we put into life we take out of it.

One true eternal success law is enthusiasm; we cannot expect to fan anything into a raging flame of completion unless we do so from the red hot, coals of our own ambition, enthusiasm and aspiration.

Power, possession, attraction, name, fame, honor, and success are all the product of a whirlwind consciousness. It is our own life stream that rushes us on past valleys, hills and mountains to deliver our possessions to ourselves, and those who do not generate energy of enthusiasm are one with the death of their own desires.

It takes a stout heart to always keep enthused in the face of prolonged disappointment and continued opposition, but it must be done if we aim to conquer. There are hours in all business endeavors, in all friendships, all associations, all loves when we must pass along aided alone by our souls' white light and as Rudyard Kipling said, "When there's nothing in us to hold on but the power (enthusiasm) which says 'hold on.'" To meet hard places on the path is a part of the great plan, and "we belong to those who go down to the sea in ships and who do business in great waters." And only those who can bid their own lives glow with an enthusiastic radiance will keep light enough to steer past the rocks in the channel.

Not everyone is equally alive in all ways, under all circumstances, and it is well that we are not or there would be no longer an opportunity to evolve on this planet, but it is possible for all of us to have a flaming sword of enthusiasm within us equal to our own development, and no matter how little it may be, it is still there, and like attracts like, for even a grain of mustard seed will move mountains.

People who let their enthusiasm awake them in the morning instead of an alarm clock will never fail in business; the managers who let their enthusiasm carry them into an interest of their very lowest employees, to see that labor is comfortable, will never hunt for laborers, nor meet strikes nor revolutions. Friends who meet their friends with interest, joy and aliveness, will count their friends by the score. And the lovers, who give being for being in perfect part, smile for a smile, truth for truth, heart for a faithful heart, will never die alone.

When we study the lives of great men and women, whether they are in the fields of government, business, science or the arts, the one common ingredient all of them possess is enthusiasm about their work and their lives. Enthusiasm enabled Beethoven to compose his great symphonies despite his deafness. Enthusiasm enabled Columbus to persuade Queen Isabella to finance his voyage of discovery and to keep going when it seemed impossible to succeed. Enthusiasm is the secret ingredient of success for the most successful people as well as the generator of happiness in the lives of those who possess it.

With the fire of a great enthusiasm within us we are burning, and we become then a torchbearer and a lamp to the feet of the slumbering multitude. We are success then because we have set the law of our own life and believing in the law we come into the protection of the law.

You are as young as your faith,
As old as your doubts,
As young as your self-confidence,
As old as your fears,
As young as your hope,
As old as your despair.
Years may wrinkle the skin
But to give up enthusiasm
Wrinkles the soul.

CONCENTRATION

Centuries ago it was written, "Whatsoever thy hand findeth to do, do it with thy might." And that subtle law of doing everything we do with our might is the very heart of the law of success. Upon concentration more than upon any other thing hangs our hope for ultimate self-perfection.

Concentration is the first step toward conscious direction and control, and without it we cannot hope to go far into the fulfillment of our own desires. Those who hope to find something to do, who have an urging aspiration and then fail to do this thing with all their might, are not fit to possess the thing for which they are longing.

It is possible to go through life idle and drifting, thinking the world owes us a living.

Yes, we do get some things because the Universal life always floats an abundance of supply on its bosom, and any one who wants to do so can eat the crumbs which fall from the idlers' table, but if we hope to come out into any definite form, use, or value, we can only do it by bending nobly to life's oars.

In life's channel there are rocks everywhere and it is our own hand that must clear the channel and our own genius that must steer us past them. Some of the most wonderful successes have been born from the genius of concentration and they never surrendered one iota of their might until they accomplished their ends.

The story is told of John W. Gates and his perfect manifestation of this success principle. He came to San Antonio as the agent of a barbed wire company, and saw the great possibilities in Texas. He expressed his belief to an old resident of San Antonio This old citizen was complaining that he could only just make a living here.

"Make a living!" said Gates.

"Any man can get rich here in ten years."

"Well," said the old citizen, "I've been here more than ten years and I have not got rich."

"Perhaps not," remarked Gates, "wealth does not hunt one up and spring from some unseen angle. One has to keep constantly on the trail, and since there are so many trails leading in the right direction in Texas, if you will keep an eye on me I'll show you how the trick is turned."

Some years later when Gates became heavily interested in the lumber business in the eastern part of the state, some one said to him: "You cannot make the lumber business go here, since there is no means of shipping it."

"Never mind," remarked Gates, "I'll make a place to ship it from and then I'll show you that there is enough lumber in Texas to weatherboard the universe."

Sometime after this he met the old man to whom he had talked about getting rich when he first came to Texas. "I hear you are making it go," said the old man, "and that you are really getting rich, as you said you would."

"Making it go," remarked the man who saw possibilities.

"Damn it! Things are making me go. Things come so easily here that I am constantly on the dodge to keep from owning the whole state of Texas. It's the easiest game I ever played. No odds what kind of a hand you have, if you bet enough you'll win."

There are thousands of failures simply because they did not have the genius to see an opportunity, but there are more failures because when opportunity was everywhere they lacked the thought force necessary to push it into form. This is not just the same as the law of "mind your own business."

There are many subtle breaks in this chain of doing and every break means failure. Living in one world and working there with our hands, while all our thoughts and wits are wandering in another, divides our forces. No one can serve two masters. Success demands that our minds shall be in all things we do, and all things in our mind, until we have established a long line of things, which we can do automatically. When concentration is complete one can do a half dozen things at one time and direct as many more. The concentrated mind does not think in concepts, it thinks in ultimates, it does not think in pennies and dollars, it thinks in millions, it does not think in cities and states, it thinks in continents; nor does it think in minutes, hours, or days but in eternities.

Here are some of the well-known failure cases we meet, and who demand help and attention. One day I went to a restaurant and after seating myself said to the waitress

"Bring me a pot of tea." Instead of bringing me a pot of tea, as I had ordered, she brought a cup of tea. She had not heard what I said. When she brought the cup of tea it was overflowing with tea, which spilled over the saucer and the table. The waitress did not know where she had gone. She was neither in sight nor finishing my order—that was sure. It is written "Thou shalt have no other gods before me" and this waitress was not doing with her might what her hands found to do. She was thoroughly reckless, careless and regardless of the thing that she was in the restaurant to do.

I have watched the people in the work world. I went into a jewelry store and the saleswoman at the counter was humming some ragtime song. Her mind was on the ragtime and she kept on singing and I hardly dared to interrupt her. When I asked for a bracelet she said, "Let me see." She proceeded to drag out some jewelry in a careless way from the shelves and continued to hum her interrupted song. Not seeing any article that appealed to my fancy, I asked, "Have you anything else?" I was simply forced to get her to pay me some attention, as a dentist forces a tooth. This woman did not know her stock, and did not care half as much about it as she did about the song. She was not there in the interest of jewelry; she was not doing what her hand found to do with all her might. She was not concentrated in her work. She was living in one world, while functioning in another.

Here is another incident of like character. I went to a coat store and asked the saleswoman to show me a coat. She stood like a statue and asked, "What kind of a coat do you want?"

I replied, "I do not know, I want you to show me some coats."

To this she replied, "Well, if you will tell me what sort you want, what color?"

In desperation I said, "I don't care. I want to see if you have anything I want."

She then walked around unconcerned and abstractedly and did not seem to know a thing about coats, yet she was selling coats, she should have known all about coats. I had no choice, but just wanted to find something suitable for me in that store.

What would a concentrated saleswoman have done? A life that was in power, a saleswoman who was doing with her might what her hands found to do? She would have said, "Here are some coats." And then she would have piled up coats of all descriptions before me and she would have made suggestions in regard to them and mentioned their attractive prices and would have tempted me to try on half a dozen of them.

The woman in the coat store was only one of ten thousand of her kind who are walking the streets out of a job, and wondering why some one else has work and she has not.

Finally I saw a coat on a rack and put it on myself and asked the saleswoman if the attached tag was the correct one, and being assured that it was I concluded to take this coat. Then I said to her, "I want to tell you that you did not sell me this coat, I got it in spite of you. Your employer would have lost this sale as far as you are concerned, and if this sale was lost, the store will lose twenty-five or thirty sales during the day because of you. And when on Saturday night the manager tells you, 'I have no use for you' you will shed bitter tears and ask what the matter is. You have not learned the first principles of keeping a position and nobody will then employ you. I am not a prophet, but I venture to say that you have been out of work half the time for the last five years, and you can't keep a place more than a few weeks." Afterward I found that I was right and that she was afraid that she would lose her place that very Saturday night.

The whole world of commerce and industry is looking for people who can come in and help them to intensify their business, who will be a help to them, they are not looking for people like this saleswoman, to stand around and let the customers buy their own goods, and sell it to themselves and almost make out their own checks. They are paying their help to be the link between their goods and the public that is seeking them, and until this is learned, people of this saleswoman type will wander and continue to wander over the face of the earth because they do not have that necessary concentration to hold them steadfast to their work. The fault is not in their employers, but in themselves. The saleswoman I have cited was one whom nobody liked. Why? Because she did not put anything into life, and consequently could take nothing out of it .I am taking this person as a principle, because she is one of many of her kind who clog the world with failure and always asking themselves, "What is the matter with me?"

Our first fundamental is that success is built upon one thing—success methods, and failure is built upon one thing—failure methods, and this saleswoman hoping for success was using failure methods and there is no relationship between them. One is the product of unconcentrated, unrelated, indifferent life, and the other is the product of a conscious, powerful, related and concentrated life.

"Do with your might what your hands find to do" and concentrate on that work until you are absolute master, no matter how much you dislike your work. If you had outgrown the thing you are doing, you would not have to do it, just as one lays down an old coat that is outgrown. The moment we are big enough to get rid of a thing, we are forced to leave that thing. We could not stay, for the larger law of our life displaces it, we cannot stay with it because the cosmic law will push it off.

Our fitness is measured by our understanding and by our perfection in the place on our path; and so today if we are working in a place that we do not enjoy, it is the measure of the state of consciousness we have intensified so highly that it cannot keep out of form.

A man once said to me, "What is the reason I always get such 'five cent' jobs? Why, I am a bigger man than that. I have a great deal of ability and I simply hate these 'five cent' jobs. I never get anything that is up to me; I can't do these little things with any degree of power or efficiency, because all the time it just grinds me to think I have these little positions. I want something that can use my abilities."

I said to him only the eternal truth when I replied. "You only have a "five cent" job because you have in you a "five cent" man whom you have intensified so that he cannot keep out of form: No man ever had a "five cent" job who had not the "five cent" consciousness and that is the measure of your concentration. This man had concentrated only in the degree of power, which represented the "five cent" man, and he will keep the "five-cent" jobs until his mind and power are enough to get more than that. He will then be the biggest man in the "five cent" position and the "five cent' job will have to slip off. It is better to be a success in a "five cent job than a failure in trying to do the work of a millionaire.

Again, women say to me: "I want to attract a great big, 'God-man' into my life. Now, what is the reason I never meet the kind of man I want to meet? What is the reason that all the men I meet are sort of 'five cent' men? They are not worthwhile." Don't you see that is the same story from the woman's side as the "five cent" man we just cited? There are both men and women who picture an absolutely matchless sort of being and then wonder at their lack of success in obtaining him or her.

The reason of all this stands out clearly. It is because the "God-man," strangely enough, by the law of God, must have a "God-woman" to mate with him. It is plain that there must be some state of consciousness in us that is intensified so that it cannot keep out of form, or we would not have attracted around us the "five cent" job or the little man or woman. Only as we pour out the whole strength of our selfhood and character can we displace these small things, and when the great bigness of our life is expressed, we then attract the position, person or object that fits that life'

When we know that no one gives to us but ourselves, and no one takes away from us but ourselves, and that we lose or gain through our own individual law of attraction, and that this attraction is based wholly on our power of concentration and ability to pass up the proofs of our fitness, then we have a new idea of success and failure. We begin to put the blame where it belongs upon ourselves—and to really know that the perfect or imperfect expression of life is in our own hands.

There is only one world, and all things are in it! They do not wait around to fall into our laps without any visible lines of transference. The tools of conquest are in our hands! Our concentrated mind, our thought force carefully directed and intensified at our own pleasure, makes us the master of our fate. No matter what our place in life may be, we can show our greatness.

Concentration first, then an unfaltering determination to do! Then, with eyes wide open.

Gates of Success swing wide, never to close again.

Out of the night that covers me,
*   Black as the Pit from pole to pole.*
I thank whatever gods may be
*   For my unconquerable soul.*

In the fell clutch of circumstance
*   I have not winced nor cried aloud.*
Under the bludgeonings of chance
*   My head is bloody but unbowed.*

Beyond this place of wrath and tears
*   Looms but the Horror of the shade,*
And yet the menace of the years
*   Finds, shall find, me unafraid.*

It matters not how strait the gate,
*   How charged with punishments the scroll,*
I am the master of my fate;
*   I am the captain of my soul.*

—INVICTUS by W.E. Henley

APPRECIATION

It is part of the higher development of all of us to learn, not only to do our own work as thoroughly as is possible, but to create the conditions and atmosphere by which all others with whom we contact, can do their work equally as well.

It is the work of us all, not only to unfold our own character and life, but at the same time to carry around with us that silent creative atmosphere which helps others to bring out and develop all that is best and desirable within themselves.

Go where we will, we find many people who must depend on other lives for the stimulus of their finer and higher growth; they have to be drawn out; they are in their shell; their sweetness and charm never find expression unless they are evoked by sincere encouragement and warm affection. The world is full of half starved lives; they go on day after day finding no legitimate expression for that mysterious something within them which cries out. There are many others who are hungry for the affection, which they often have, but never receive or possess, because those who hold it for them never give it voice.

Again, there are many who have possibilities within them of a very high order, but those possibilities remain undeveloped because nothing in their lives, and no one around them, brings out these latent powers. There are some who can only express in the warm atmosphere of appreciation. William James, the eminent American psychologist stated the deepest urge in human nature is the craving to be appreciated.

Many individuals throw out an atmosphere of chill instead of appreciation; they are totally unaware of the influence they throw out. There are many, many lives that go around antagonizing everyone they meet; driving friends and friendships from them; defeating their hearts' dearest purpose, and never understanding why, when it is plain to those who look on, that all their difficulties come from a lack of thought about the delicate and intricate adjustments of human life.

There: are thousands of homes, which are without sunshine and good cheer, not because they are really without love, but because they have missed the one line of transference of these things and that is, appreciation and the expression of the appreciation.

There are thousands of offices, stores, work-shops, factories, schools, and places where humankind beat out their lives, that are wholly without inspiration, not because they are lacking in earnestness, but simply because they have never formed the habit of recognition and have none of the cooperative appreciation which gives out to others and at the same time brings out the best for itself.

Companion with this lack of appreciation is the spirit of sullenness, crankiness, and complaint; a continual looking at the dark side of things, and a sourness which makes not only one's own atmosphere acid, but reaches out into the lives of all those around us.

It is time for us to learn that we should have sunshine of our own and also that we have no right to steal the sunshine away from other lives. The world is often a beautiful place to other people until some one, with no appreciation or recognition, steals it from them. *We have no more* right to enter a life and rob it of its joy, than we have to enter a house and rob it of its valuables.

It is small enough for us to look at the gloomy side of life and never feel the force of appreciation, but it is still worse to make our atmosphere so dense with it, that we crowd our discontent and heaviness into the lives of others around us.

Of course we may be a crank if we want to be; that is our own affair. But we have no right to crowd our smallness into the lives of others, and neither have they any right to allow us to do it. We should all be taught to recognize such disagreeable natures and atmospheres at a glance, take them as a signal of undevelopment, and protect our own lives from them. Some time in our life we all meet one of these walking frosts and we never forget the chill they always give us, until we learn our true position toward them.

Whenever we feel all of the meanness of our undeveloped nature welling up within us, it is a good plan to just keep it to ourselves, and cultivate the appearance and atmosphere of recognition. After a while we displace the chill by the sunshine we have willed into expression. If we conquer it a little, day-by-day, we will soon cease to have it. A smiling face, a happy life, a soul full of appreciation which shines and radiates from us; this is the proof that the soul offers to the world that it has learned how to create its own kingdom.

We should train our eyes to see the good, the true, and the beautiful in everything, and then recognize it by every avenue of expression. It is not always enough to a life that we think it is good or great; we should tell the life what we think.

"A little word in kindness spoken,
  a motion or a tear
has helped to heal a life that's broken,
  and made a friend sincere."

When a life needs encouragement, give it. Don't see its limitations, even though they almost overshadow its power; help it to grow into what it believes it can be. Encouragement is only another name for appreciation. It is no harder to see the good qualities in others than it is to see the faults, and it is a whole lot more comfortable for everyone. Life is a continual process of selection, and since we cannot choose but select something, learn to make it from the beautiful and best qualities, and then hold them up before the eyes of the possessor and see it with all the high lights of love and appreciation turned upon it. If we make the most of all the good and great things we find in our lives we will have very little time left to grieve about what we do not have.

When we go into a store and find all the clerks, who wait upon us, cross, distraught and uncivil, don't report them to the proprietor; that will never cure them. Just treat them yourself by appreciation; give them sunshine; pour out all the warmth of yourself upon them and watch the effect. It won't be five minutes until the effect begins to show; just the tones of your voice can start a new vibration. Do not be afraid to express your appreciation of them or for anything they do for you; there is no life on earth that can stand against real sincere recognition.

When some one answers us in a hateful manner, don't answer them back in the same tone; stop a moment, give them a thought of warm love and a kind word and see the storm clear away. There is no force on earth higher than the constructive energy of appreciation, warmed by a great love. There is a latent spark in every being that flares up in answer to the stimulation of appreciation; and the knowledge and use of this power widens our lives and our field of usefulness. The whole business world everywhere is clamoring for live, vital workers, who can attract and hold the outside world. It pays big salaries to those who can prove themselves in whatever work they represent, but there is positively no place whatever for the "dead ones"; they already glut the market.

Appreciation; the power of sincere recognition of our abilities and capabilities; and side by side with it, the same approval of other lives; these are all factors in the foundation of a life success which cannot be fully understood until it is tried.

You need not be effusive in expressing appreciation. A sincere acknowledgment of how you feel about the work done, the service rendered, or the pride you have in a specific accomplishment is enough. Nobody ever tires of receiving sincere appreciation.

If your appreciation is for a long-range, continuing activity, periodic expressions of gratitude are appropriate. To tell your husband or wife from time to time how much your life together has meant to you and how you appreciate the little things he or she does to make life more pleasant will enrich a marriage.

Appreciation must be sincere. You have to really feel and believe what you are saying for it to come through to the other party as sincere. Insincerity cannot be disguised by fancy words. Your voice, your eyes, your body language all reflects your true feelings.

In order to get real appreciation, we must get real love into our hearts and then teach ourselves how to connect with our words. We may manufacture a grin and an artificial approval, but at the same time we must be getting the real thing into our inner being or there will come a time when our words will be only as sounding brass or tinkling cymbals.

There is a great truth in the power of thought transference, and it is just as easy to create a mental atmosphere of appreciation, as it is to speak it; and for some lives this is sufficient to encourage them, but be wise and know when the spoken word is necessary to complete their character.

Live appreciation; radiate it; let it shine through you, but by all means learn to make your lips declare the truth your heart has known. Encourage people; tell them of their good qualities of mind and heart and person too; it will revive them; make them think they are understood; perhaps awaken hope and will and power to do; and when this is finished be sure that we recognize and appreciate all that others do for us.

To aid others in developing to their uttermost and to "dare to be what they will to be," is the great testimony of our capacity of controlling, directing, and completing our own life.

There is no power so impressive, so strong for success, so powerful in life building, and so certain in its everlasting benefit to mankind in general, as this one great human attribute—appreciation, or the power of universal recognition.

Then each life is great in itself and increasing in its greatness with others. Then life and love and God are one.

HATEFUL COMPARISONS

Comparison, both true and false, takes part in our success and failure. Comparison is everywhere on our pathway. One would have to be born with a supreme ego never to compare oneself with anyone else, or with certain opportunities and lack of opportunities of action. "By the mistakes of others wise men correct their own," and unless we are proud and self-arrogant we must find splendid opportunities of measuring our own ability with the ability or lack of ability of others.

Strong, positive ideals are necessary in the building of a perfected selfhood, and positive ideals are bound to keep one in a condition of comparative thinking, for only as we see the ultimate self clearly can we hew to the line along the path of our true development. There are always those who can do the very thing we are doing and do it in a different way and better, perhaps, than we are doing it, and no matter how fine we are, we would own method the methods of those who are our masters.

A master consciousness and a master expression is always to be emulated, and those who do not know this and who stands fast bound to their own peculiar method, refusing to entertain even the idea of a change in their method, are cads and snobs, who will meet their own defeat through their own egoism. They may be all right, but so is a world of others and it will do them good to take notice.

Not all of perfection is expressing through anyone all at once; no matter who we are or what we are doing, we must grow into it out of the natural states of our thoughts, feelings and actions.

All art, literature, music, drama, commerce, politics, and industry have their living pictures of perfection and there follows, as incentives, ideals and examples to help bring out in us all that is capable of stimulation.

Healthy, normal, and careful comparison of our own ability and our own expressions with the highest type of these things we can find in others, will keep us on the keen edge of finer effort and spur us on to accomplish still greater expression in action, and as long as we keep to this we are under a success law which cannot be broken.

Around this true law of healthy comparison there swings the negative destructive law of hateful comparisons. Hateful comparisons have ruined fine exemplary lives.

Filled with a desire divine to be perfect in the thing it is doing, possessing a supersensitive nature, seeing the magnificent expression of others in the same work and comparing their own feeble effort with the fuller perfect one, they have sunk down in despair and given up all effort. Instead, all that was needed was a little longer practice and steadfast application, keeping what they had, and without hateful comparison, using the expression of those who were their masters as examples to inspire them, instead of becoming discouraged and giving up all effort.

Hateful comparisons have become the cankering worm in the heart of the finest tree of life, and it works its way through the most minute things and where we would least expect. There are many stories one could tell of it, but here is a plain case of failure through hateful comparison:

A woman wanted me to dine with her. She said, "I want to have a long talk with you and I want you to tell me just what is the matter with me. I am not happy, we are not as successful as we should be, and my husband seems discouraged, and I seem to annoy him more than I comfort him, and yet I do not know just where we are slipping off the line, but I know we are slipping."

I dined with this woman and her husband and this is what I found: The husband was a commercial traveler, very successful, clearing an enviable yearly salary. They had been in many countries and at last had selected a certain city for their permanent location. They decided to build a little house, just to have an abiding place to which they could repair for rest during his vacations, and where the wife could remain while he was away on short trips. It all seemed right and the most sensible thing to do.

I was the first guest in the new little house. The house was a perfect gem in architecture and all the appointments were perfect and I exclaimed with delight at the beauty and simplicity. As soon as we were alone together the wife said, "Now come and see all of my new house." Then and there she began to reveal the canker at the heart of her rose tree of life. Comparisons—hateful, small, belittling comparisons! She began at the hall; the rug had to be excused—it was not good enough, but all that she could have then, but oh, there was a rug she really wanted and one of her friends had such a rug. The beautiful rug on her own floor was lost in her senseless regret of comparison of what she wanted and had not. Every room in her house came in for the same hateful comparison—the pretty curtains in one room were valueless because they were not some other kind of lace; the dining room table was carved and beautifully done but worthless to her because it was not pure mahogany. Every room was blasted and made desolate by her belittling unconscious comparison. Even the dear little maid who served the dinner came in for her hateful comparison; she, too, was worthless when compared with some foreign maid she had had abroad. Then the husband—hateful comparison was rampant there. He should have developed himself to command more salary. Other men, who did less work had better positions and commanded bigger salaries. Everywhere this wife turned in thought she compared his work, himself and his salary; she pulled him down and destroyed every citadel or shrine he had ever put up in his own life. Naturally I found the husband silent and inclined to say, "what's the use," and with a sort of stolid "hang on" atmosphere that had in it the whole story of the cause and effect of his wife's unconscious failure law.

After dinner she took me to her own pretty boudoir and seating ourselves cozily she said, "Now, go on, tell me, just what is the matter with me." Of course, I told her in terms too plain to be misunderstood for she was a growing soul and could stand the truth.

Hateful comparisons were dragging down her self esteem, and dulling the keen edge of enthusiasm in her husband, and she had always been his whole inspiration. She was unconsciously putting out his light and this silent destroyer was watering their growing lack of success. She recognized her error and began rebuilding at once, and they are today more than successful, happy, and contented with the things their own efforts provide, and she remains his inspiration and he her lover-husband.

Just one more example: Every day I hear persons say: "I won't sing if they do," "I won't try to do this or that if so and so is going to be there," and day after day, in some way or other, persons are destroying themselves by their senseless, hateful comparisons.

No one can ever hope for success by this means. Individual success is built on the self, and the power of the self to retain its selfhood. *Be your self!* Do the thing you can do in your own way, no matter how any one else does things, you have something they have not, and that is your own originality; they may know all you know, but they do not know just how you are going to say it—that is your secret and your success.

There are no two blades of grass alike; God made infinite variety, just so there should not be hateful comparison; there is, in truth, no such thing as "comparison." We are each perfect for our type and different from any one else's. "Let the wild rose alone, she couldn't be the lily if she tried," Ella Wheeler Wilcox said, and you are all right, no matter what your expression may be. If you work on, perfecting your own type, you will get somewhere, but if you bind yourself with the wretchedness of comparison, you will fail, just because you make your consciousness one with the law of failure.

Whatever you have around you in things, people and conditions are just what you have the power to create, and they will remain until you change them by making new conditions, so don't belittle them or compare them—love them and call them good and try to displace them by finer attraction. Jesus said, "And I, if I be lifted up, will draw all men unto me," and people who will perfect their individualities will have success; it will come and abide with them because they are fulfilling the true laws of their beings.

Comparisons for growth and example—these are only embodied stimulation to higher effort and purpose and are the ladder by which we climb past our dead selves to higher things. Comparisons for depreciation and rejection of our finer selfhood—this is failure—and those who do it reap what is sown.

The true self knows, and knowing, dares the way, turning aside, perhaps, to get a shorter path, but holding fast to the great mortal birthright that allows it to say, "I am that I am."

HAPPINESS

There are those who are always sad, unhappy. Their gloom reacts on everything around them and carrying this load of despair they become a dread to their friends, their loved ones, business opportunities pass them by because no one wants a walking tale of woe which, by every look, tells to every passerby the negative failure method of their lives.

If we look deeply into every life that touches our own, we will find that each one is on the same journey; each is hunting for the same object. It is plain that everybody is filled with only one great purpose, which stands paramount to all others, and that is, the desire to be happy, to find happiness, not the fleeting content which any one can feel for an hour, a day, but that all sufficient, certain and abiding contentment which makes for peace, power and plenty at every point in our human existence.

Watching this search for happiness we cannot help but ask, "what is happiness?"

"Where is it to be found, and how do we recognize a life which has found it?"

There are many definitions for happiness, but it seems that the only real answer is to say, "happiness is found by simply getting what we want." There are grades and grades of happiness, for there are grades and grades of desire. The soul which desires, then realizes that desire and which knows that every other desire which it may ever have, will also be realized, is the one, and the only one, which can say it has found happiness.

From ancient times people have been taught that self-denial was the first law of our beings, and that with "renunciation life began." This has led humanity out into an endless concentration along lines of lack and loss. Half the world believes it cannot have what it wants.

Today we do not believe that teaching and know it never was meant to be what the world intended it to be. Today we know that we can be what we will to be, and that God wants us to have everything we want, and will back us for every desire of our lives. We know that happiness is the law of life, and our natural condition; that unhappiness is a disease and the sign of a life astray from the Infinite union.

We believe in God now more and more, because we believe in ourselves more and more, and we see always something in our every action that speaks of Him and His infinite care. Today we do not lay down our desires and try and try to say "Thy will be done" but we know that our will is His will, and we can say with an exaltation of spirit that it is His will that we meet His will, and we can meet it unafraid.

Happiness and unhappiness are conditions of the mind and have nothing to do with real life.

Life is full of curious contradictions, all set in motion by our own and other peoples' ignorance, and it is the position we assume toward these conflicting forces which determine whether we shall be happy or otherwise. It is no one's fault but our own if we are unhappy; it is no one's fault but our own if we are sick, poor or full of lack. The whole scheme of existence makes for happiness and all life is full, complete, serene, only awaiting our own awakening to that fact.

There are always two ways of looking at these things which we want, and which we think are necessary for our happiness. One is to determine whether from our viewpoint we consider them attainable; and if we are convinced that they are, then secure them; but if we are convinced that they are not, at least, without great striving and resistance on our part, then lay them down and let them alone for that time, get over want them until life brings them into our current. We must never forget that substance is always changing, and so is position, and the unattainable of today may become the attainable tomorrow, just from the fact that the law of supply and demand are equal.

We can never hope to possess anything until we feel and know that it is directly in our line of transference, and it is our own folly if we sit down and become unhappy over it, while we recognize its separation from our lives. As soon as our wills recognize that it is not our own, we put it beyond our reach for that time; we will never get it until time, and our own wills, bring it into our atmosphere.

There is no use striving after anything, there is no use grieving for it or mourning over it. This is true no matter how much it may seem to contradict our early teachings; we simply cannot get anything by running after it and straining every nerve to secure it; we only secure by attracting and polarizing ourselves above the plane of competition, where we can become conscious creators. When we have discovered this, we have come into knowledge of how to get our true position to universal substance, and our own desires can get what they want; through this we demonstrate our own desires on the physical plane, and manifest the true freedom.

In order to be happy we must learn not to put a perverted value on life's differentiations. It is in being influenced by these things that we get unhappiness. We have absolutely nothing to do with the differentiations of people, place or conditions. We are only responsible for one thing in this life, and that is *ourselves;* everyone else is responsible for themselves and do not need to worry about us. If we would only learn this, and refuse to put our hands on another's life, and not allow their domination in our lives, we would go a long way in this search for happiness.

It is not our own lives that make us unhappy, *it is our fear of what others will think of us.* We will never become happy nor know true happiness until we learn that it really does not matter what any one thinks of us. There is only one true criterion of our actions, and that is *ourselves.* The only one we are responsible for is ourselves; it is impossible for us to tell what is needed in our development save ourselves; no one can tell us what to do. In the last analysis we must stand alone, and if we learn this, we put ourselves and our affairs far beyond the reach of promiscuous direction into the great path of truth, where and whatever is, is right for us as well as for others.

The life that has found its own center and who knows that it is its own unaided law that stands amid eternal ways in the midst of changing and chaotic conditions, that walks serenely with mind alive to the divine teachings, has the Success law, and the true position toward the differentiations of life and the changes of substance. It is poised above the plane of competition, where it has only to desire and speak the word, and it will clothe itself in physical manifestations for it. Does it want wealth, it knows the opulence of supply and asks for it. Does it want wealth, love, possession, anything—it knows that there is abundance everywhere, and in the calm purpose of life, it has only to ask and it is given. This is realization, this is happiness; a realization which only is vouchsafed to those who have made a conscious union with the Infinite.

The life that sublimes itself into the plan above the human thought-plane of error comes into the "perfect peace that passeth all understanding," for it has touched the Absolute; that life looks at all the conflicting expressions of this earth life with all seeing eyes, and knows that no matter what the expression, the self-made loss, the self-made pain or remuneration, the hand of the eternal Good is guiding this life finds peace and happiness, and this brings power and power brings Success. It knows that every idol of our human hearts must somehow, somewhere be laid down unless we know how to take it with us as we pass onward to our own fulfillment. It knows that we must lay it down with tears and pain, and lips dumb with suffering, and leave it until in that great day of all days, our soul is born into the higher kingdom of thought, where we learn to make union with our own, through God-like consciousness.

True possession is true happiness. We cannot lose anything that is our own. It is true that whatever we really desire and vitalize into existence for ourselves, may become our own, not only now but also for all eternity. Failure, loss, pain and grief are but words to the life that has awakened to this knowledge.

It keeps its soul filled with the greatness of growth; looks at attainment from a grand pinnacle of feeling where pain, trouble, heartache, loss and unhappiness are unknown, but the happiness of an eternal realization is its soul. And happiness is a magnet attracting to itself all the free wonderful things in the world.

POISE

Poise is the quality of the human mind that makes for perfect balance in all of life's relations. It is activity under control. It enables one to pass from end to end of the pole of human feeling and function normally at every point of contact. It means health in sickness, life in death, silence in strife, hope in despair, joy in sorrow, pain in loss, and everlasting and eternal Good in the face of evil.

Poise is to the human soul and body what the compass is to the mariner. It is the cloud by day and the pillar of fire by night to the soul adrift on the psychical ocean; it is one expression of the highest energy. When every other hope has failed, the soul that has poise is not altogether desolate.

Sensation is the direct cause of action; we are continually receiving sensations through mind, soul and body, and acting accordingly. Those of us who can receive every sensation of our daily life, and regulate ourselves to vibrate with it no matter how high or low it may plunge us, have a poised life and are masters of ourselves. It is said all the world falls into line with those who declare themselves masters. This is true, and only those who have learned the lesson of true poise command the unpoised. Poised people are positive people, and the negative world must obey their will.

What constitutes a poised and an unpoised life? Simply this: The understanding and use of will power, the application of natural laws to every phase of life, and the correct position toward everything on all planes. Everyone is possessed of just much will power, which by training and study may be increased to an unusual amount.

Given a certain amount of this quality, it is easy to see that those who understand and use their will power increase their growth on all planes far in advance of those who do not know or refuse to know their true worth. It is also easy to see that the greater the development, the greater the controlling power becomes and the more certain of results they may become, because they have learned the inherent power of their own being.

A will power that is halting, full of fear, and uncertain of its own creations, cannot hope for success in the activities of life. The changing substances of life with which we are obliged to cope make it impossible to intelligently direct our plane unless we have taught ourselves that fine balance which cannot be altered by external conditions. Sickness, old age, poverty and death are only examples of loss of poise; it begins with weakness of the will and ends with atrophy. Sickness and poverty are inherited and acquired, and one of our safeguards against them is to poise ourselves in a positive physical and mental attitude and thus control our own being by refusing to be made the host for a crowd of emotions we do not enjoy. Inherited disease can never manifest unless we recognize the legacies that dead people have left us and accept them; they are negative conditions and can have no power over us save that which we give them.

Acquired sickness is a condition purely of our own making. Even accidents cannot happen for those who are poised in the Infinite vibration of truth, since those only who are poised for just those things which they choose and want, can come to them.

In our will lies the power to create the diseases or to destroy them; there are only two important points through which disease, gains entrance to our bodies, and these points are our emotions and our minds.

Our emotions sense a purely imaginary condition, and our wills send these imagings through our bodies in thought currents until the minute cell-brain of our bodies receive them and register them in their consciousness until they can reproduce them in form.

Just here is where our poise comes into action; it is time for us to recognize that we are masters of communications which our minds will telegraph to our cells; our wills inhabit degenerative thoughts, and whatever our minds receive may be distributed evenly among the receiving stations of our nervous systems and no one center paralyzed by shock.

There are those who are so separated from this will power and control that a sudden surprise or shocking news will render them unconscious, and in others reason has gone out, and even life itself. All these grades of emotion are rates of vibration and poise is one of the highest rates of vibration known. The soul that has found its poise and its true power and position toward the changing conditions of life, has stood face to face with that supreme poise which masters all, and it has faith to say "though I walk through the valley of the shadow of death, I will fear no evil."

We are all acquainted with unpoised people—self-conscious, negative creatures; those who "don't know" and who say "I can't." The whole world is full of a great skulking apologetic crowd, who cannot even come into our presence without carrying with them the atmosphere of begging to be excused for being born. This is the expression of the unpoised, and it is they who have caused all the trouble between labor and capital in the world, and will continue: to cause it until the "I" in all these individuals is lifted up and placed where it should be by themselves. It never occurs to them that they can brace up and look the whole world in the face; and that they do not have anything they do not want; they do not know how to say "no" and will never say "no" to things unless they *will*; they simply go on allowing themselves to be bullied to death by stronger wills, which would gladly everything they want if they knew how to get it; they whine, groan and curse, and then strikes and bombs tell the rest of their unpoised story.

Poised people do not need any of this, in fact, they will not accept it, they are strong and creative; they know what they wants and how to get it; they are not influenced by outside talk; they have inborn right of purpose; they are neither sick, poor nor down-trodden, simply because they refuse to be; no sweat shops for them, and if they ever run one themselves it is because they, like a thousand others, sees this great world full of unpoised human lives in which they can traffic, which seems only fit to be sweated, and because they, with others of their kind, have not learned that greatest of all humanitarian lessons—"as ye did it unto the least of these, ye did it unto me."

The power of poise is great when used for evil; it is Divine when directed toward the uplifting of self and the race.

The first step toward poise is to cast out fear. There is nothing in all the world of which we need be afraid; we must know this, say it, feel it and live it until it stands out in our lives a part of our every action and we have passed into mental freedom. Be sure that we are the highest expression of life on this plane and have absolute dominion over our lives; we must never waver in our mental mastery; after we have secured our own freedom, set about getting it externally; we can have what we want and what we want is the very best thing for us to have. It is our consciousness trying to get into expression; do not let anyone else think for us, we have to become our own masters before we can have any force with any one else; advice is all right but it does not amount to anything only as it helps us to reach our own conclusions.

Do not let us worry about what anybody will think of us; no person is our friend and no person is our enemy, but all people are our teachers. We may do as we please, it is not really any matter what any one thinks but ourselves; if others do not like what we do, let them leave us; we want companions in our life work not slaves, servants or masters.

The only thing that we are ever really responsible for is ourselves; it is our business to lift up the "I" until association with it will lift all others up. Do not think it is a dangerous philosophy to teach that we all shall do just what we please. Far from it, for in doing what we want to do, we find the greatest of all lessons—that there is one great and continuous universality of life, action and being; and when we always do as we please, our inborn sense of right will teach us to never do anything that is not for our own good and the good of the world at large. We will find the greatness of happiness in doing what we want and we will want the whole world to be happy.

Absolute perfect union with our own selves and common sense relations to all external life; belief in our own power of accomplishment and our own Divine right to be "what we will to be," faith, hope, love toward all others and that great world-wide charity that "thinks no evil,"—this is poise, and as we learn it on the human, physical plane of expression, we pass into the unseen psychic world of laws and become one with that great invisible world-poise which never fails. Poise in the human conscience is the deep spiritual fulcrum through which man can pull his own material universe into form poise in the center means power outside and poise and power become the foundation for a success that is eternal.

THE RULES OF THE GAME

There is a game called life
Which we all know;
Some play it with wide-open eyes,
While others risk their all upon one throw,
And throwing, lack the craft to load the dice.

This throwing and lacking the craft to load the dice is the failure side of effort, and the winner in the game is the one who plays with a complete and perfect understanding.

Every game has rules; there is not the simplest thing in the world that is not governed by its own law, and to learn how to operate this law is the game that is played everywhere.

The thing we call "life" is a master game, and those who understand all the rules of life are winners in just the degree that they plays fair. They may cheat and lie and shift their hands and win for a time, but the universal master of the game checkmates them when, in some unguarded moment, they lay down their hands.

There are great eternal rules in the game of life that must be regarded, and we violate these rules at our peril. Before we can begin to study the rules we have to learn that one-half of life is wholly dependent upon humankind. "The Lord hath need of thee" is written, and universal consciousness is everywhere waiting for humans to manifest it. God has long since finished His work in this sphere. He waits now for the extending mind of humankind to receive and express the wider reaches of Divine intelligence.

When we awaken to the first knowledge of the game of life and study the rules, we find four great rules set, and no amount of questioning; resistance or denial ever changes them. We can kick against them if we will, but our game grows less and less successful the longer we play it by other rules than the first rule of life.

These are the four great rules in the game of life, and we must master them if we ever wish to succeed.

FIRST: *"Thou shalt have no other gods before me."*

SECOND: *"As a man thinketh in his heart, so is he."*

THIRD: *"Resist not evil."*

FOURTH: *"Ask and ye shall receive, seek and ye shall find, knock and it shall be opened unto you."*

No matter where we go we find the failure world playing this game of life by every rule but the right one. "Thou shalt have no other gods before me," the sky soul said, and yet the million of gods before which half the human race bows and worships, and from whom they beg assistance they tread the self-same paths their ancestors trod who knew not God—they know not God. They have rested their whole hope in human powers and endowed human things, and conditions with all sorts of imaginary powers, enthroning them in their hearts and lives, surrounding them with impossible attributes, then, when the true law of these things becomes revealed, they are broken and desolate; they lose because they failed to play the game fair; they are the product of their own misguided interpretation.

Out in the world of disease and lack, poverty and heartbreak, these people wander, the hopeless example of the laws they served! The hospitals are full of diseased, suffering ones, the insane asylums overflowing, surgical sanitariums receive a never-ending line of incurables telling him who runs and reads how imperfectly they understood the law.

"Thou shalt have no other gods before me," but before them and between them and their God-source stands—the personality of the doctor, the crutch or the drug, the hope in the sanitarium, the belief in the surgical knife—pinning their life to these things they grew farther and farther away from the divine spark of power within them. Resting their hope in people and things, they lost the conscious union with the great creative spiritual energy of the universe which, set in active operation by the true rules of the game of life, would have prevented their physical degeneration. False to the universe; success in health, false to themselves; evading the true law of success in health; they become the worked-out sentence of their own judgment, and they themselves are discards from the universal pack.

In the world of material gain, commercial and industrial success, this law of violation of the true rules falls with as sure a blow as it does in the flesh. "Thou shalt have no other gods before me," and yet here struggling for supremacy people seek to rise through the power and influence of their peers. They look for help everywhere but to the true source within themselves and the universal; they think other people can give and that other people can take away, when the true rule is that no one but ourselves can do this. When we link ourselves with the universal and create our own in consciousness, it passes to us by divine law; it is the great universal rule of the game of supply. If humans can give, then humans can take away, and those who work with this belief in their hearts, are playing false to the true rule and must fail, for they build this law for themselves. Those who rise through the power and influence of another has only passive possession, and must somewhere surrender everything that is not their own, and pass it into the higher law of active possession. No one can take our own away and our own is just what we create for ourselves, and we create it by recognizing it in the universal, and then looking to others to bring it to us or connect us with it.

"Thou shalt have no other gods before me," and all mine is thine, and those who forget that their source of supply is universal, and not personal but who links their lives with the personal will have to fight their way through to the end until they become the example of their own game of life.

Here is a story, homely and unadorned, which shows the full measure of the transgression of the true rules of the game of supply. A certain woman owned a chicken farm and took keen delight in feeding the chickens. One of her primitive observations was this: She said that she would take a big pan of feed to the chickens' yard and set it down right in the center in easy reach of the hens. Then this was what would follow: A few hens would be first at the pan and getting their mouths full of the good things in the pan, would run away to the corner of the yard; then the other remaining hens would come up and seeing the hens with their beaks full of food would run after them, and pretty soon there would be a scramble all over the yard, hens struggling with hens for the tiny scraps in their mouths, picking, fighting, while the flowing mess, was standing untouched in the center of the yard waiting for the return of the angry fowls.

The woman said, "These chickens are just like humans out in the world, fighting to take the little human possessions from each other, while the great universal waits with its opulence to give to any one who comes." And again, she said, "If they had emptied the pan I was ready and willing to get another panful, but they wore themselves out scrambling over the bits."

No truer tale ever was told and when we play the game of supply by such false rules (and we do so every day) we must fail because it is the inevitable end of the game.

We are receivers, creators, and distributors, and must play our own perfect part of the universal game. God, the great Universal Life, has provided some better things for us, that they, without us, cannot be made.

The second rule is equally important. In the bible we are taught: *"As a man thinketh in his heart, so is he" (Proverbs 23:7),* and yet the weary failure world goes on every hour thinking fear, anger, resistance, condemnation, poverty and disease. There is little hope for a final winning in the game if with every move players break their own law of power. Faith is an all-abiding necessity according to the universal rule: Faith in God, faith in the human race, and faith in our own power: To think the thoughts which will give ourselves everything just as we would have them—this is the great command, and "there is not a thing in all the world but that thinking makes it so." What folly it is to spend our hours thinking of everything in the world that we do not want, when with another thought move we can change the whole game for ourselves and for others.

The failure world is saturated with doubt, fear and uncertainty; "I can't" and "I don't know" are their devils, they haunt their sleep and follow in their waking hours. The game of life is spoiled because with these things dogging their footsteps they lose the memory of the true rule, and their hearts are filled with thoughts that become things of fear or evil, and dwells with them.

The failure world always asks for a certainty before it will accept or consent. The success world fills its heart with thoughts of the thing it desires and lets these thoughts build it into a divine faith in the ultimate. *"As a man thinketh in his heart, so is he,"* and those who have to have a certainty before they venture, have lost before they begin, because there is nothing on this planet that is sure but changes—the one great changeless law of change will carry the law of success or failure through to its own end.

The third rule—*"Resist not evil."* This rule demands persistent attention, and until one learns the higher laws of life and finds that there is really no evil but that which we call evil is only unripe good. We will be continually in conflict, and conflict is one of the paths to failure; there are so many things that seem wrong or so impossible that one must have a consciousness as high as Heaven to hold it all good and right. Yet the Universal Rule of the Game of life was this "Resist not evil:" "Do good to them who despitefully use you—If a man smite thee on one cheek, turn to him the other also."

In all the multitude of lives seeking for higher self-attainment, thousands forget this rule, they play by the rule of their own benighted consciousness—"An eye for an eye; a tooth for a tooth"—and as the game goes on they find that they have won and lost. They have won their game, perhaps, but have lost love, and without love they are but as "sounding brass and tinkling cymbals." They have gotten even with those who are their enemies, perhaps in the human way their vengeance has been satisfied, but there is the mystic law and the higher rule of the game which said: "Vengeance is mine, I will repay" and they failed while they seemed to prosper. As the days go on they learn the fateful lesson that we can never really "get even" with anyone—that our enemies are the instruments in the hands of our own law which we have endowed with power over us, and that when we think we are getting even with our enemies we find that we are settling old scores with our own soul. And it is not to them we have to answer, but to the Universal Rule and that has said, "Resist not evil." Living a life of hate, resistance, condemnation and vengeance is playing off the universal law, and in order to fill our own true part there must be born in us understanding of life in the highest, the knowledge that the one life in all and through all; then love will take the place of resistance—love for God—love for humankind—love for ourselves, and success born of love is eternal.

The Fourth Rule. *"Ask and ye shall receive, seek and ye shall find, knock and it shall be opened unto you." (Matthew 8:7)*

Faith without works is dead, and the one who wants to play the game of life to a tremendous finish must work! Jesus said "My Father works, and I work" and the very first thing any one does who wants to be truly successful is to work for some one else quickly. The Universal Rule sets us at work at once. Ask—make known your desires in work, deed and thought; do something. "Whatever ye ask, believing that ye will receive, that shall ye receive." The Divine Intelligence takes every life at its own estimate, but in the face of this first great commandment we do not ask, we do not seek, we do not knock the great law of service. It is unknown in our lives.

Every day we speak out of our hearts' desires. If we listen to the words of the failure multitude we will soon learn that by their words they are justified and condemned. They say, "What's the use?" "I know I can't," "There is nothing in it for me." "There is no use trying, I have tried and failed, I know I can't get it." "Nobody will help me," "business is awful," "I expect that I will lose," "I shall not try any more," "I am too old," "I hate life." Yet the rule of the game says: "Ask, seek, knock," but standing just before the doors they have closed by their own ignorance they turn away and in despair say: "I've played out, the game was never fair."

The success of life means to gird on the whole armor of God-consciousness and to go out into the battle field, and move things into shape with a power born of a knowledge of the game. When we take our wants out into the multitude, and having asked the universal, ask those also with the poise born of this higher authority, they will hear and heed and become then and there a direct line of transference between us and our own. Then, listening to those around who are asking us, we fulfill the rules of service, and as we go on seeking wider and deeper fulfillment of our desires, we can knock at the door of the hearts of others and they will arise and bid us enter.

The universal rule says, "I have set before thee an open door no one can shut." The only part of the game we can make perfect is to open the doors of life around us. As we go on playing our part in unison with the universal rule, we come ere long into perfect mastery, our hand no longer lacks the craft to load the dice and our throw is swift and sure because we are one with the law.

Unity—one with all, "No other God before"—but God in all and through all the universal rule in all things and all things in the universal rule, recognizing always the infinite source.

Faith is so boundless that it is past all doubting, for it knows in what it puts its trust.

The human quality that can wait—and with nothing before and nothing behind—still knows that it is the divine thinker of its own thoughts, and that *as a man thinketh, so is he.*

Love born of an understanding deep as life itself, reaching out for the distraught faltering human heart, loves on through doubt and darkness until the impossible becomes the possible through the inspiration of love's own spark. *Ask! Seek! Find!!*

Walking the world path of the human, serving the wants of others as links to our own, knowing that the highest love of God is service to others, asking of all, seeking everywhere, knocking at every door, striving to give of all we have to those who have not, and then when we face arrears turn back into the universal for our own increased supply—this is the square of success and around these play all the other laws. The one who digs into wisdom and builds on these rules has dug deep and built a house of success on a rock and though the storms of life come, it will not fall.

Unity, Faith, Love, Service—this is the perfect foundation! Four-squared the city, of life stands. This person is one with the Great Master player of the Game, and has learned that this game called "Life" is not a coward, best, that one only wins who plunges in and in and while playing, prays.

COMPENSATION

"I am so weary of toil and tears;
Toil without recompense, tears all in vain."

Do you know that this is the cry all over the world? No matter how much any one may appear to have, no matter where one stands in name and place, deep in almost every heart there is this cry of loss and tears, this story of bread cast upon the waters which has not returned.

"Give to the world the best you have and the world will give back to you" has not been made good in every life according to its own story. Most of us know those who have spent their lives in loving service, yet something which they cannot understand and over which they have no control, deals out to them blow after blow until at the end of life they lie down to die with no pay for any effort of their lives. They gave to the world the best they had, yet, viewed from their confined paths, the world never repaid them for their giving.

Then there is another class whose lives seem to be peculiarly free from suffering, and who seem to have the things they want without putting forth any effort to secure them. They live their lives care free; they never give of their store nor of themselves; they lie down to die with a calm unruffled peace, showing no fear of the past and no concern of the future. They have hoped nothing, feared nothing, given nothing, and they go back as ashes to ashes, and dust to dust.

There is yet another class who give and receive, whose lives are beautiful, whose ways, are "ways of pleasantness, and all their paths are peace"; their lives are one long round of loving service, a giving and receiving, which has had no beginning and no end, but always is.

What makes the difference? Is it true that there is toil without recompense? Do we sow where we can never hope to gather?

New Thought says no, it cannot be. It is an unwritten law that desire is the prophecy of its fulfillment; the law never takes one thing away but something is given in return.

There is no such thing as wasted effort. It has been written, "with what measure ye mete it shall be meted unto you." The answer to this great loss and gain is within our own being. We always get what we concentrate for, and the conditions. Around us are the objective answers to our own prayers. Matthew Arnold said: "Ye suffer from yourselves; none other binds ye that ye weep and die." People who pledge themselves to a certain action, a certain development, get that thing and all the other things that go with it, of which they were unconscious when they signed away their freedom. The law takes each of us at our word. There is no coming in at a later hour and saying,

"Oh, I did not mean it." The die has been cast. The threads carry out the pattern.

Let us look at the question of compensation from an everyday practical standpoint. Do we want to become artists, actresses, physicians? Then the first thing we do is to consecrate ourselves to that work; the next thing is to begin along the line we have chosen. If an actor or actress, we bear the poverty, the disappointments, the hours of toil and hardship, the chagrin and despair, until in some unexpected moment the compensation draws near: the time of our service ends in a larger service which we have bought for ourselves by our consecration, If we want to become artists, it is the same story, the hours of useless labor (when viewed from the world's position), the wasted daubs, the mistakes, the hours of waiting for public approval, and at last the goal. The same thing holds good in every field of labor, but the soul, which has fully felt the consecrating power, never lays down the struggle. It follows the beautiful vision of its inner senses. There are many, whose lives have never reached the sweet land, which they saw by promise, but they have been recompensed for their work by just the joy of doing.

There are those who have given years of work and study to bring about a certain development and have lain down and died with all of their work apparently unfinished; yet the coming, following generation learned from their efforts, their work was not lost, for by the steps they cut, others climbed the peaks of glory.

We must learn, too, that we can make no demand on the world in any way with any hope of realization, if we are not prepared to supply equal value to the world with the gift of ourselves.

Consecration is the first step, then the way begins; that our feet stumble and our hearts bleed is but a condition of the way brought about by our ignorance. The soul that consecrates itself to service realizes its desire, but it must pay the price for such, and the human price of service is often toil without recompense as measured by our mortal comprehension.

No matter what we want, we will find that we can get it if we are willing to pay the price, not always in our way, but in the way that will bring us towards the thing for which we have asked. Left to our own way we would now and then go in a directly opposite path from our desires, for we cannot see the end from the beginning, but once we have made the consecration, if we find the path rough and winding, we cannot choose but go on.

Compensation is eternal in the universe. We get what we ask for. If we mourn our supply it is because we do not understand the causes which we have set in motion and are expecting perfect returns from imperfectly formulated plans.

Those lives, which seem so destitute of compensation, are not really, so they have only made a mistake in interpreting it. In order to understand compensation, we must understand cause and effect, and know that we only reap what we sow. The life which sows for service reaps service; for knowledge gets knowledge; love gets love; there is no escaping the harvest, but we do not always recognize the compensation for it does not come to us invariably in the guise we expect.

I know of a life that sowed love, kindness and gratitude to another life for fifteen years and at the end of that time was robbed of honor, name, place, position and everything that heart holds dear, by the hand of the one whom it has served so well.

Compensation! No, indeed, but do you think those years of faithful loving service were lost? Never; they could not be; they were charged to the Universal supply and had to be cashed in by that life somewhere. In the later years a stranger in another life brought back to this life the harvest of loving kindness and crowned it with joy, peace and power. Compensation made perfect, only in another form.

Compensation is always near us, but often we do not recognize it as our own; it may meet us in a new garb at any turn in the lane of life, but while our eyes are blinded with hot tears of loss we cannot see it. We sow our seeds of desire and the purple flowers of pain blossom around us while we look in pained surprise for the white rose of our expectations. We have not learned that "like attracts like" and that on the path the law is made perfect.

We limit our compensation by our habit of renunciation; we have not yet dared the full splendor of what we may possess. We allow ourselves to think that in order to grow we must renounce; that one thing is sacrificed for another to be gained, when if we only knew, it is the all will that we can take every desire of our hearts with us to the path, make them one in the one life, and reap our harvests from them all.

Some will say, "I cannot have money and education, so I gave up the hope of ever getting rich in order to attain knowledge." Another says, "I cannot serve two masters, so I renounced the life of pleasure for that of service." Oh, the pity of it! Don't you see where they went wrong? They gather at the harvest what they sow, and there is no reason why they should not have gathered the fullness of all their desires if they had only known.

The life that sows service, pleasure, joy, peace, money, power and every hope of its soul, will gather the compensation of its sowing in some way or another, day by day, because it is the unchanging law of the Infinite substance. The human mind has limited itself; it has distorted the soul vision and forgotten the eternal promise "seek and ye shall find."

To plant for the highest matter of growth, look deeply into your own lives and find out just what you want, and then ask yourselves if you are ready to pay the price for it? If you are ready, then consecrate yourselves to it and all that the consecration brings, and when you are looking for returns or recompense, be sure that you recognize your own when it comes. Do not limit yourselves; take with you into this consecration everything that you want, and then do not complain of what you are called upon to pay for your gifts. Whatever comes to you in this consecration belongs to the path you consciously chose; do not give up, but turn again and again in loving consecration, and soon you will come to that place where love of, or care for, compensation ceases, everything becomes a labor of love, or only the "work of Him who sent you," and toil and tears will be swallowed up in the joy of Divine compensation.

> *"Unanswered yet; nay do not say ungranted,*
> *Perhaps thy work has not yet all been done.*

> *That work began when your first prayer was uttered,*
> *And God will finish what He has begun.*

> *If you will keep the incense burning brightly there,*
> *His glory you shall see, some day, somewhere."*

CPSIA information can be obtained
at www.ICGtesting.com
Printed in the USA
BVHW042258210420
578043BV00009B/279